# OUR LIFE WITH JESUS
## Teacher's Manual

# OUR LIFE WITH JESUS

Teacher's Manual

Faith and Life Series
BOOK THREE

Ignatius Press, San Francisco
Catholics United for the Faith, New Rochelle

Nihil Obstat:     Rev. Thomas M. O'Hagan, S.L.L.
                Censor Librorum
Imprimatur:    + Joseph T. O'Keefe, D.D.
                Vicar General, New York

Director: Rev. Msgr. Eugene Kevane, Ph.D.
Assistant Director and General Editor: Patricia I. Puccetti, M.A.
Writer: Sister Mary Catherine Blanding, I.H.M.

Catholics United for the Faith, Inc., and Ignatius Press gratefully acknowledge the guidance and assistance of Reverend Monsignor Eugene Kevane, former Director of the Pontifical Catechetical Institute, Diocese of Arlington, Virginia, in the production of this series. The series intends to implement the authentic approach in Catholic catechesis given to the Church in the recent documents of the Holy See and in particular the Conference of Joseph Cardinal Ratzinger on "Sources and Transmission of Faith".

# CONTENTS

Introduction . . . . . . . . . . . . . . . . . . . . . . . . . . . . . . . . . . . . . . . . 7

1. God Loves Us . . . . . . . . . . . . . . . . . . . . . . . . . . . . . . 15
2. God Created the World . . . . . . . . . . . . . . . . . . . . . . . 19
3. Learning about God . . . . . . . . . . . . . . . . . . . . . . . . . 22
4. The Promise of a Savior . . . . . . . . . . . . . . . . . . . . . . 25
5. Abraham: The Father of God's People . . . . . . . . . . . . 28
6. The Prophet Moses . . . . . . . . . . . . . . . . . . . . . . . . . 30
7. King David . . . . . . . . . . . . . . . . . . . . . . . . . . . . . . . 33
8. God's Laws of Love . . . . . . . . . . . . . . . . . . . . . . . . . 36
9. Loving God Most of All . . . . . . . . . . . . . . . . . . . . . . 38
10. The Lord's Day . . . . . . . . . . . . . . . . . . . . . . . . . . . . 41
11. Obedience and Love . . . . . . . . . . . . . . . . . . . . . . . . 43
12. Purity and Truth . . . . . . . . . . . . . . . . . . . . . . . . . . . 46
13. God's Tender Mercy . . . . . . . . . . . . . . . . . . . . . . . . 48
14. Meeting Jesus in Confession . . . . . . . . . . . . . . . . . . . 51
15. The Christ Child Is Born . . . . . . . . . . . . . . . . . . . . . 55
16. Jesus Grows in Age and Wisdom . . . . . . . . . . . . . . . 58
17. Signs and Wonders . . . . . . . . . . . . . . . . . . . . . . . . . 61
18. The Last Supper, Our First Mass . . . . . . . . . . . . . . . 64
19. Jesus Gives His Life for Us . . . . . . . . . . . . . . . . . . . 67
20. Offering Gifts of Love . . . . . . . . . . . . . . . . . . . . . . . 69
21. The Holy Mass . . . . . . . . . . . . . . . . . . . . . . . . . . . . 73
22. Offering Jesus to the Father . . . . . . . . . . . . . . . . . . . 76
23. The Bread of Life . . . . . . . . . . . . . . . . . . . . . . . . . . 78
24. Jesus Comes to Us in the Holy Eucharist . . . . . . . . . . 80
25. Jesus Rises in Splendor . . . . . . . . . . . . . . . . . . . . . . 83
26. The Coming of the Holy Spirit . . . . . . . . . . . . . . . . . 86
27. God's Family on Earth . . . . . . . . . . . . . . . . . . . . . . . 88
28. Our Life in the Church . . . . . . . . . . . . . . . . . . . . . . . 91
29. Mary, Our Mother and Queen . . . . . . . . . . . . . . . . . . 94
30. The Communion of Saints . . . . . . . . . . . . . . . . . . . . 96

Appendix . . . . . . . . . . . . . . . . . . . . . . . . . . . . . . . . . . . 99

# INTRODUCTION

# A Note to Parents and Teachers

## ABOUT THIS SERIES

The *Faith and Life Series* has many features which make it unique among catechetical programs. There is one in particular we wish to mention.

If you turn to the first few pages of *Our Life with Jesus* you will notice immediately that it is written on a reading level higher than that of the average third grader. This is intentional. We believe that children of this age deserve to hear more of the Good News of the Catholic Faith than a "Dick and Jane" reading level would permit.

This approach has several advantages. It is obvious that in the early grades a child's oral comprehension is far beyond his reading ability. For example, an eight-year-old can follow the plot and dialogue of a T.V. program even though he would find the written script of the program unintelligible. Applying this principle to catechetics, the *Faith and Life Series* presents Christian doctrine in a style designed to arouse wonder and challenge the intellect of the child, thus avoiding the boredom that is often fatal to catechetical efforts.

In addition, we all know that children love to be read to. As they listen to the narratives in the *Faith and Life Series* children will learn to associate God with the joy of storytime rather than the drudgery of a reading lesson. All too often children perceive the study of their faith as simply one more "subject" to be set aside with relief when they leave the classroom. By lessening the emphasis on reading we wish to help concentrate their attention on the Gospel message itself, and thus see the faith not as schoolwork, but as divinely revealed truths that have a bearing on every aspect of their lives.

All those who have worked on the *Faith and Life Series* sincerely hope that it will provide parents and teachers with the assistance they need in the task of evangelizing young minds.

# Principles

## TEXT AND GRADE LEVEL

The third-grader has just completed a year of preparation and study for his First Communion and confession. The third-grade text, therefore, aims to continue and strengthen the child's understanding, love, and appreciation for the sacramental life.

The third-grade child can concentrate longer than the younger children, but still depends greatly on his senses and needs to see, hear, sing, draw, etc. This text incorporates both the longer attention span and the dependency upon the senses as it aims to help the child practically express his love for God through the sacramental life and exercise of virtue.

## CATECHESIS: NATURE AND PURPOSE

Because of your willingness to share your time and talent, you have entered more fully into one of the Church's most important and sacred duties, that of making Christ better known and loved by his children, young or old. This duty of the Church entails handing on the message of God, in its entirety and purity. You cannot mix God's message with political or social views without betraying the Divine mission. Political and social trends come and go, but the word of God is always timely. Catechesis must be based on Revelation as transmitted by the universal Teaching Authority of the Church, in its solemn or ordinary form (CT 52, cf. *Dei Filius* chapter 3). The doctrine you hand on by your teaching is received by your students as it truly is, the very Word of God, accepted as it is taught, namely, on the authority of God revealing (cf. 1 Th 2:13). This teacher's manual is designed to help you in this important work of handing on the living and unchanging Word of God.

Catechetics, according to the *General Catechetical Directory*, is the form of the ministry of the word of God, "which is intended to make men's faith become living, conscious, and active, through the light of instruction" (GCD 17). This instruction presupposes that the student already knows and believes in at least the basics of the gospel as taught by the Church. A good way to determine the depth of your students' knowledge of the faith is to ask them the basic questions listed in the Appendix. It will then be easier to know which students require more fundamental instruction.

## THE CATECHIST: CHRIST'S INSTRUMENT

If teaching religion seems like a big task, that is only because it *is* a big task! But don't get worried! As Pope John Paul II said in *Catechesi Tradendae:* "It is Christ . . . who is taught . . . and it is Christ alone who teaches" (CT 6). This statement means that you are Christ's instrument; through you he will spread his message. You have a very important role in faithfully passing on the message of the gospel, the constant, unchanging message: Jesus Christ, the only begotten Son of God, made man. On the other hand, you also have the assurance that God is going to help you every step of the way in proclaiming his message. You, too, have the guarantee given to the apostles: "I will be with you always even to the end of the world" (cf. Mt 28:20).

You are also very important because it is the living catechist, the living example, who gets the message across. No matter which text you use, no matter which method you choose, it will be the message you present, your living of the gospel, your likeness to Christ that will be most important in bringing your students closer to Christ (cf. GCD 71). Consequently, you need to prepare yourself for the task, always confident that if you do your part God will do his. The best way to prepare yourself is to pray, to study, to pray, to plan, and to pray.

## THE ROLE OF THE PARENTS: THE FIRST CATECHISTS

The family provides the first and irreplaceable introduction to Christian faith and practice for any child. Parents are the first instructors of their children. The instruction in the faith, which starts from the earliest age, should include not only the parents' good Christian example, but also a formation in prayer and an explanation and review of what their children have learned about the faith from methodical religious instruction and liturgical events (CT 68). (In some situations where the children attend neither a Catholic school nor a CCD class because these are not available or are inadequate, the parents [or the grandparents] are the *only* source of catechetical instruction. If this situation is yours, God bless your efforts and may this series help you in the children's formation in Christ.)

Parent cooperation is very important to a teacher's success as a catechist. You should try to involve parents in their children's instruction: sharing with them the program and methods you are using, consulting them about better ways to reach their children or to help with problems that may arise. Let the parents know that you are there to help them fulfill their duties in forming and educating their chilren in Christ (cf. GCD 78, 79).

# Practicalities

## LESSON PLANNING

Lesson planning is very important for an organized and successful teacher. It helps you cover all the material systematically in the time that you have available.

The first step in planning is to make an overview of everything you want to teach during the year. For example, there are thirty chapters in the third grade text, but suppose you are in a CCD program and you are going to have only twenty-eight classes during the school year. You will need to plan which lessons you can combine and which lessons you might want to expand over two or three weeks. If you have the students every weekday, the overview is also helpful to you in scheduling what needs to be covered every week so that nothing is left out or covered too quickly. Included in the Appendix is a chart to help you plan your course for the year.

The second step is to plan the daily lesson so as to reach the students on as many levels as possible. The *General Catechetical Directory #70* mentions *experience, imagination, memory,* and *intelligence* as different faculties of the children that should be active in the task of learning. A good lesson plan will involve all of these faculties.

## RECOMMENDED CATECHETICAL SOURCES

*Catechism of Christian Doctrine,* published by order of Pope St. Pius X, trans. Rev. Msgr. Eugene Kevane (Arlington, Va., Center for Family Catechetics, 1980). (The questions in the children's texts are from this catechism.)

Hardon, John A., S.J., *The Catholic Catechism* (New York: Doubleday and Co., Inc., 1975), 623 pages.

Lawler, Ronald, O.F.M., Cap., Donald W. Wuerl, and Thomas Comerford Lawler, editors, *The Teaching of Christ: A Catholic Catechism for Adults,* 2nd ed. (Huntington: Our Sunday Visitor, Inc., 1983), 640 pages.

*The Roman Catechism,* translated and annotated by Rev. Robert I. Bradley, S.J. and Rev. Msgr. Eugene Kevane (Boston: St. Paul Editions, 1985), 586 pages.

*Sharing the Light of Faith,* National Conference of Catholic Bishops (Washington, D.C.: United States Catholic Conference, 1979).

*Vatican Council II: The Conciliar and Post Conciliar Documents,* gen. ed. Austin

Flannery, O.P. (New York: Costello Publishing, 1975).

*Vatican Council II, More Post Conciliar Documents,* gen. ed. Austin Flannery, O.P. (New York: Costello Publishing, 1982). (This volume includes *Catechesi Tradendae,* and the *General Catechetical Directory,* both vital documents for the Catechist.)

## POINTS ON TEACHING CHILDREN

1. The first thing necessary for successfully communicating the message of the gospel is to have a genuine love for the gospel and for your students; all else flows from this love. A genuine love consists of desiring the greatest good for your students, which necessitates maintaining a fair and consistent discipline. Your task is not merely to teach a subject matter but to form children in the image of Christ. State clearly your requirements and the reasons behind them. Do not let the rules slip. If you have made something a policy stick to it! Jesus himself was gentle but firm.

2. Learn the names of your students as quickly as possible. This small effort will help you maintain discipline and let your students know that you care enough about them to remember who they are.

3. Try to call on everyone, not just on those students who volunteer: in this way everyone remains attentive and the shy students have an opportunity to come out of themselves.

4. Give clear directions for assignments. For example, do the first part of the assignment with the children or do the assignments or activities yourself beforehand so that you are familiar with the problems your students might have. Walk around the classroom so that you can give individual attention to those students having difficulties.

5. If you notice a normally attentive student not paying attention, find out what the problem is and be willing to take the time (outside of class time if possible) to help or find someone who can.

6. When using the chalkboard, remember to start at the left-hand side. Skipping around is extremely confusing for the students.

7. Overplan. It is all right if you run out of time; it can be a disaster if you run out of material to teach.

8. Review the lesson with your students at the end of the class period and review the lesson again at the beginning of the next class before starting the new lesson. Repetition *is* the mother of learning.

# Suggested Introductory Lesson

**Aims:**

To find out how much the students know and understand about their faith; to get to know the students and to familiarize them with class content and procedure.

**Materials Needed:**

Student texts and activity books, folders with students' names on them (optional), name tags (optional), seating chart (optional), game or quiz (see the Appendix for game), paper and pencils.

## Procedure

1. Pray.

2. Play a name game to learn your students' names, or give them name tags, or make a seating chart beforehand.

3. Hand out text and activity books. (You might supply your students with folders in which to keep books, papers and pencils.)

4. Ask the basic catechism questions from the Appendix, either in the form of a quiz or a game.

5. Introduce the subject the students will be studying during the year.

6. Assign the students Chapter 1 of the textbook to read. (You might find it more practical to have the reading assignment read and discussed during the class covering the particular chapter rather than assign it as homework.)

7. Pray.

# CHAPTER 1

# God Loves Us

---

**Background Reading for the Teacher:**

Lawler, pp. 29–43 (second edition).
Hardon, pp. 53–63.
St. Teresa of Avila, *Way of Perfection,* chap. 39 (an explanation of the excellence of the Our Father).

**Aims:**

The students should be able to identify God and his perfections; to see that God is One who loves each of them from all eternity with infinite love; to identify the soul as distinct from the body; to define the doctrine of the Trinity; and to understand the importance of communal prayer in general and the Our Father in particular.

**Materials Needed:**

Chalkboard, chalk, poster paper, paste, magazines for picture cutouts, a "treasure" for a simulated treasure hunt, paper, pens, three candles, crayons.

---

## Activities

1. Complete the Activity Book assignment for Chapter 1.

2. Give a chalk talk.

3. Discuss God's perfections. Show pictures of or describe things that remind you of God's power, holiness, wisdom, and beauty, such as a thunderstorm (power), saint (holiness), teacher (wisdom), or beautiful landscape scene or attractive person (beauty). For a five-day presentation, assign the students to bring in pictures reminding them of God's perfections. Have students paste the pictures on poster paper and be ready to explain why they chose them.

4. Discuss God's loving knowledge of his children. Read aloud the section from the third paragraph of Chapter 1: "This God was thinking of you. . . ." Then ask your students, "How does this

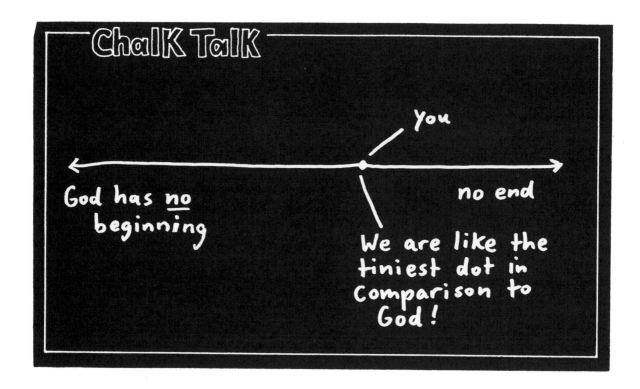

**ChalK TalK**

you

God has <u>no</u> beginning

no end

We are like the tiniest dot in comparison to God!

make you think and feel about God?" Have them write a prayer or draw a picture to describe how they feel in response to the truth that God has loved them from all eternity. Afterward, allow the students to share their responses with their classmates. ("Johnny, will you come up and read to us your prayer?") For some students, you may want to read their responses for them, or you may choose to forego this exercise.

5. Simulate a treasure hunt. Hide a "treasure", such as a candy bar or other item that you know your pupils will enjoy; let them look for the treasure. (Be sure to pick a hiding place that is not too difficult, so you can go on with class.) "Why is it exciting to look for a treasure?" (Let them answer.) "How many of you have been on Easter egg hunts?

Why are you excited to go on an egg hunt? We should be just as excited or even more so with our truest and best treasure, who is _____." (God) "Open your books and read the section starting with 'Our best treasure is God himself . . .' Why is he our best treasure? In what ways can we go on a 'hunt' for God?"

6. Tell a good joke or relate a funny story. If you have none, ask one of your students. (There is always a joker in every class, from kindergarten to senior level!) Be sure to get the students to laugh. Now ask, "Why are you laughing? Can your pet dog or cat or your fish laugh? Why not? You can laugh and they cannot because you have a *soul*, which makes you see funny things. What else can the soul do? Read the paragraph starting with 'God loves you

so much that he made you in his own image . . .' What happens when you die?'' (The soul separates from the body.)

7. Explain the doctrine of the Trinity as simply as possible, drawing three circles united in one circle, etc. If you are teaching a five-day presentation, ask your students to bring you things that remind them of the Trinity. Bring to class three candles. Have three students each light one candle. Then put the three candles together to have the three flames make one flame. Three flames in one—a symbol of the Trinity. Relate the story of St. Patrick and the three-leaf clover. Perhaps the children can find one and bring it to class.

8. Talk about the prayer the Our Father. It is very important that your students do not just recite prayers mechanically. Be sure to explain each line and how very important each request is, since Jesus taught us this prayer. After your explanation, have a "poster display". Direct seven groups of students to make posters of the seven lines of the Our Father. Example: One group can do posters on the line "Our Father, who art in heaven" etc. After the posters are completed, hang them up in a display case at your school or in your classroom.

9. From the very first lesson, direct your students to make up a prayer chart like the one below.

| Name: | | | |
|---|---|---|---|
| | *Morning prayer* | *Our Father* | *Night Prayer* |
| Monday | | | |
| Tuesday | | | |
| Wednesday | | | |
| Thursday | | | |
| Friday | | | |
| Saturday | | | |
| Sunday | | | |
| Check off each time you say your prayers. Bring the card to your teacher at the end of the week. | | | |

Check the prayer charts. Give the students stars or holy cards when they are faithful to these prayers.

10. Have a communal prayer service. Use the missalettes.

11. Quiz your students on the questions at the end of the chapter.

**Lesson Plan for a One-day Presentation**

1. Pray.

2. "Welcome to third grade! You had such an important year last year, because you went to confession and received Holy Communion. This year we are going to think about these two sacraments and how we can continue growing in love for Jesus."

3. Give the Chalk talk; see activity 2.

4. Show pictures or describe things that remind us of God's perfections. See activity 3.

5. Explain to the students about God's love for each of them.

6. Explain the Trinity, especially by using the blackboard and telling stories.

7. Direct students to pray the Our Father together. Then explain its importance and meaning.

8. Review basic concepts of Chapter 1.

9. Assign students to make a prayer chart to bring to class next week.

**Suggested Schedule for a Five-day Presentation**

1. God and his perfections
   *Aim:* to identify who God is and what his perfections are; to develop a closer relation to God as love; to foster daily prayer by making and keeping a prayer chart.

   *Activities:* see activities 2, 3, and 4. Assign students to bring in pictures or descriptions of things that remind them of God's perfections. Do a prayer chart (activity 9).

2. God and his perfections
   *Aim:* to identify and appreciate God's perfections.
   *Activities:* see activity 3.

3. God as our one treasure; the soul
   *Aim:* to help students see the longing they should have for the precious treasure of divine life; to identify the soul as distinct from the body.
   *Activities:* see activities 5 and 6.

4. The Trinity; the Our Father; communal prayer
   *Aim:* to define the doctrine of the Trinity; to appreciate this doctrine as a supernatural mystery.
   *Activities:* see activities 7, 8, and 10 (8 might extend for two days).

5. Review; communal prayer service
   *Aim:* to review this week's material and/or to have a communal prayer service.
   *Activities:* review game, quiz. For prayer service, see activity 10.

# CHAPTER 2

# God Created the World

**Background Reading for the Teacher:**

Lawler, pp. 43–56.
Hardon, pp. 69–78.

**Aims:**

The students should be able to define and describe Creation; to understand that everything God created is good; and to identify God's purpose for men and women.

**Materials Needed:**

Blackboard, chalk, poster paper, crayons, magazines with pictures of nature, copies of *National Geographic,* flashlight.

## Activities

1. Complete the Activity Book assignment for Chapter 2.

2. *Creation.* Ask the students, "What is the difference between saying, 'Let there be fudge brownies' and making fudge brownies?" (When you say "Let there be . . ." snap your fingers or do something to indicate you want it done immediately.) "How is this difference similar to God's creating and man's making?"

3. *Creation.* Turn off all the lights. Ask your pupils, "What does it mean to be in darkness?" Start reading or have a child read the fourth paragraph on page 11: "First God said . . ." As each created object is mentioned in the reading, hold up different representations, starting, of course, with light. (It might be enjoyable to first turn on a flashlight and then the larger lights.) Pictures of sparkling sea, land, and so on will be helpful. It might be better to have the students draw on poster paper the different representations (sea, land, birds, man and woman). Something else to add to the drama is to ask someone at school with a very deep voice to read the part of "God".

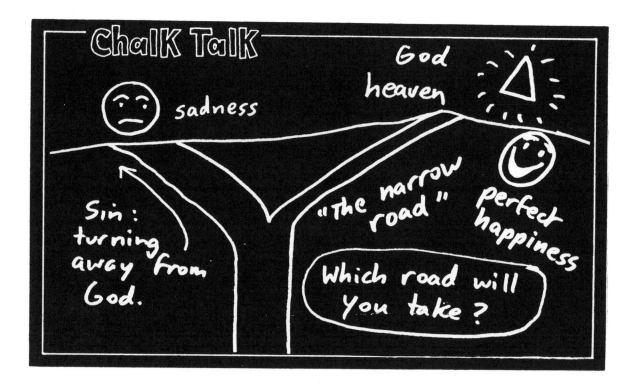

4. *Creation.* Bring many magazines that have pictures of nature. Ask the students to look for a picture that shows beautifully God's goodness. Also show the students pictures from a magazine such as *National Geographic* and tell them very simply about some of God's natural wonders, showing forth his goodness and love.

5. Make up a "Litany of Creation" in which the children thank God for all his gifts. For example:

   For the sun and moon, we thank you, Lord;
   For the snow and rain, we thank you, Lord . . .
   Etc.

6. Give a chalk talk.

7. Ask each student, "What is your very favorite thing in the world?" (horse, pet dog, baby brother, baseball games, etc.) "Now, tell us how these favorite things come from God and show forth his goodness."

8. Be careful to explain the meaning of sin. Read aloud the section on sin (fourth paragraph on page 13).

9. Tell stories of saints who have had "glimpses" into heaven, such as St. Thomas Aquinas, who said "all is straw in comparison to what I've seen", or St. John Bosco, whose mother appeared to him from heaven.

**Lesson Plan for a One-day Presentation**

1. Pray.

2. Review chapter.

3. Explain the teaching on Creation by doing activities 2, 3, 4, 5, and 7.

4. Do the chalk talk on the purpose of man in activity 6.

5. Explain how horrible sin is; see activity 8.

6. Tell stories of heaven; see activity 9.

**Suggested Schedule for a Five-day Presentation**

1. Creation
   *Aim:* to define and describe Creation.
   *Activities:* see activities 2 and 3 (3 should take a while, since you should direct the students to draw their own representations or cut out pictures).

2. Creation
   *Aim:* to appreciate the goodness of God's Creation.
   *Activities:* see activity 4.

3. Creation
   *Aim:* to appreciate Creation.
   *Activities:* see activities 5 and 7.

4. Man's creation
   *Aim:* to identify God's purpose for men and women.
   *Activities:* see activities 6, 8, and 9. Also do an in-class reading.

5. Review
   *Aim:* to review this week's material.
   *Activities:* review game, quiz.

**Notes:**

# CHAPTER 3

# Learning about God

**Background Reading for the Teacher:**

Lawler, pp. 199–210.
Hardon, pp. 40–50, 541–543.

**Aims:**

The students should be able to review the doctrine of Creation; to identify the way God helps us to know him, namely, through the Old Testament, his Divine Son, Tradition, and Scripture; and to see the Pope as the good shepherd of the Church.

**Materials Needed:**

Blackboard, chalk, poster paper, crayons, costumes for skits, pictures of the Pope, Bible stories for children, filmstrip projector.

## Activities

1. Complete the Activity Book assignment for Chapter 3.

2. Direct your students to write messages to their closest friends. "Why do you like to write or to talk to people you really like? How is this joy like the joy God has in telling us about himself?"

3. Give chalk talk A.

4. Discuss some parables.
   a. Tell some of Jesus' more familiar parables out of a "Bible Stories for Children" book.
   b. Act out several parables. (the rich man and Lazarus, Lk 16; two sons, Mt. 21; the judge and the widow, Lk 18; the Pharisee and the publican, Lk 18; the woman in search of her lost coin, Lk 15) Get costumes for your students—old sheets, pillows, etc.) (see Appendix).
   c. Direct the students to make up their own parables. Allow them to tell their parables to the class, pretending they are like Jesus and the class are his disciples.

5. Give chalk talk B.

# Chalk Talk Ⓐ

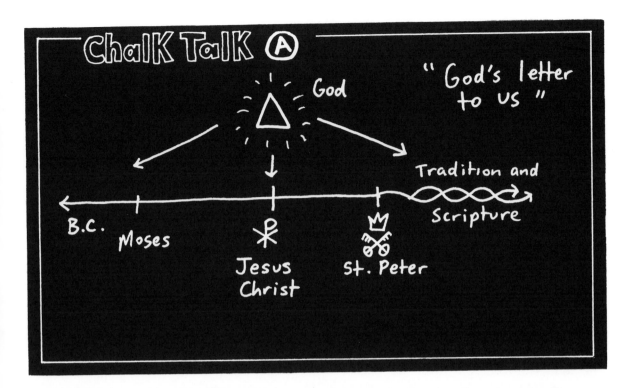

God

"God's letter to us"

B.C.  Moses  Jesus Christ  St. Peter  Tradition and Scripture

# Chalk Talk Ⓑ

Key to happiness = T and S
Tradition and Scripture
(The way we come
to know Jesus Christ)

6. Show a filmstrip on parables.

7. Show the children pictures of the Pope. Also go over the role of a shepherd and how the Pope is the shepherd of our Church.

**Lesson Plan for a One-day Presentation**

1. Pray.

2. Review chapter.

3. Explain how God helps us to know him through the Old and New Testaments. Read aloud the third and fourth paragraphs on page 15 of the student text. Give chalk talk A, in activity 3.

4. Go over the importance of parables. Tell a famous parable of Jesus.

5. Explain the importance of Scripture, Tradition, and the Pope. See activities 5 and 7.

**Suggested Schedule for a Five-day Presentation**

1. God communicating with his people
   *Aim:* to identify and to appreciate how God communicates with us through natural and supernatural means.
   *Activities:* reading of the first two paragraphs and discussing activities 2 and 3.

2. Jesus and his parables
   *Aim:* to understand the importance of God's own Son communicating with his people; to appreciate the use of parables.
   *Activities:* see activities 4a and 4c; prepare for activity 4b (prepare costumes and so on).

3. The use of parables
   *Aim:* to appreciate the use of parables.
   *Activities:* see activity 4b. (This may be done for the last lesson; you may wish to work on the plays daily for a small portion of the time.) See activity 6 (filmstrip).

4. Tradition, Scripture, and the Pope
   *Aim:* to identify the role of Scripture and Tradition; to see the Pope as the good shepherd speaking for Christ.
   *Activities:* see activities 5 and 7.

5. Parable plays or review games and test
   *Aim:* to review this week's material.
   *Activities:* see activity 4b (it may be enjoyable to invite other classes or, better yet, the parents of the children, to see see the parable plays).

**Notes:**

# CHAPTER 4

# The Promise of a Savior

**Background Reading for the Teacher:**

Lawler, pp. 43–66.
Hardon, pp. 83–99.

**Aims:**

The students should be able to define the concept of angels and to identify their role; to identify the creation of Adam and Eve and the doctrine on the fall; to identify the promise of a Savior; see the role of baptism in the life of grace; and to see the importance of growth in grace.

**Materials Needed:**

Paper, construction paper, crayons, blackboard, chalk, cardboard, aluminum foil, bowl of water, baby doll.

## Activities

1. Complete the Activity Book assignment for Chapter 4.

2. Give a chalk talk about angels.

3. Tell the story of of the battle of St. Michael versus Lucifer. To make this battle more vivid to your students, instruct a few of the boys to act it out. Have a narrator, a St. Michael, and a Lucifer, along with good angels following St. Michael and bad angels following Lucifer. Let them "fight it out" with cardboard swords made of aluminum foil (see Appendix). Also, put cardboard wings on the good angels. Add horns to the devils and haloes to the angels (good) and you have enough excitement for the week! Make sure the narrator tells about the battle and its "ongoing nature".

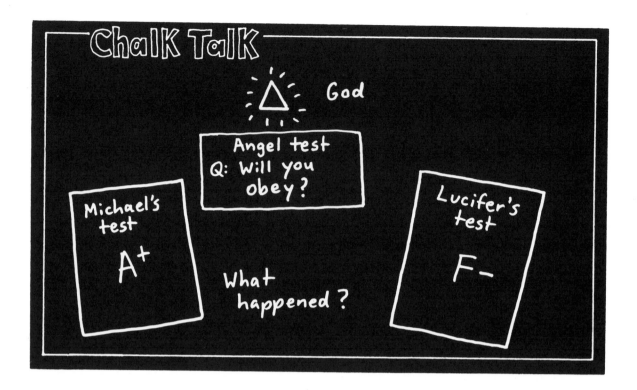

4. Talk about the story of Adam and Eve.
   a. Direct a play featuring Adam, Eve, and the serpent.
   b. Before and after: make up masks (see Appendix) showing a happy face of Adam/Eve and sad face of Adam/Eve in order to illustrate the happiness before the fall and the sadness following the fall.
   c. Direct your third graders to draw pictures of what they think the Garden of Eden before the fall might have been like. Also instruct them to draw pictures of the sadness after the sin of Adam and Eve.

5. *Light of the World.* Turn off all the lights. Light a large candle. Ask the children, "What are you looking at? Why? How is this like the people of God in regard to the Savior?" Turn on the lights. Read aloud with the students the second paragraph on page 21 in their texts: "God punished Adam and Eve . . ."

6. Act out a baptism. It might be helpful to have a doll that the "godparents" can carry. You might try asking your parish priest to come in and speak about baptism and then act out one. Another idea is that of pretending to baptize in an emergency. At any rate, it is important for you to instruct your students to appreciate the value and beauty of baptism.

7. Talk about tests and temptations. Instruct your students to make up "tests" and temptations they go through every day. You might tell them that, just as Adam and Eve were put to the test, so each one of us has tests of love, which we can either fail or pass.

Examples of tests for third graders:

| "Pass" | "Fail" |
|--------|--------|
| Doing my assignment well and not sloppily | Doing my assignment sloppily |
| Picking up my clothes in the morning | Not picking up my clothes |
| Obeying immediately | Not obeying immediately |

**Lesson Plan for a One-day Presentation**

1. Pray.

2. Review chapter.

3. Do the chalk talk about angels in activity 2. Also point out what angels are (see the first paragraph of page 19 in the student text).

4. Tell the story of Adam and Eve. Show pictures of Adam, Eve, and the Garden of paradise. You may want to illustrate with the masks (see activity 4b).

5. Ask your third-graders to make up "tests" that they undergo each day. Write their suggestions on the board. Correlate their tests with the test of Adam and Eve. See activity 7.

6. Compare natural light to the light of the Savior. See activity 5.

**Notes:**

7. Explain about baptism and the importance of growing in grace. If you have time, simulate a baptism so your students will better understand how to baptize.

**Suggested Schedule for a Five-day Presentation**

1. Angels
   *Aim:* to define the concept of angels and to identify their role.
   *Activities:* see activities 2 and 3.

2. Angels
   *Aim:* to identify the battle between St. Michael and Lucifer; to pledge to be loyal to God, as was St. Michael.
   *Activities:* see activity 3.

3. Adam and Eve
   *Aim:* to identify the creation and test of Adam and Eve and the doctrine of the fall.
   *Activities:* see activity 4.

4. The promise of a Savior, baptism, and grace
   *Aim:* to identify the promise of a Savior, to see the role of baptism in the life of grace, and to see the importance of growth in grace.
   *Activities:* see activities 4, 5, 6, and 7.

5. Review
   *Aim:* to review this week's material.
   *Activities:* review game, quiz.

# CHAPTER 5

# Abraham: The Father of God's People

---

**Background Reading for the Teacher:**

Lawler, pp. 76–80.

**Aims:**

The students should be able to identify God's sending his messengers to remind his people of his promise; to understand and appreciate Abraham's obedience to God; to understand the importance of Abraham's faith.

**Materials Needed:**

Paper, blackboard, poster paper, crayons, popsicle sticks, felt, construction paper, cutout paper, large shoe box.

---

### Activities

1. Complete the Activity Book assignment for Chapter 5.

2. Stage an exercise on "waiting". On the board, draw a large circle and place the time as 4:00 P.M. (or an hour after school lets out). Ask several children to demonstrate how tiresome waiting can be. (Let them be as funny as possible.) Ask your students, "How do you feel when you have to wait for a late ride? Why? We easily get tired of waiting. How can we compare this to the chosen people?"

"Please open your books to Chapter 5. Let us read the first paragraph."

3. Talk about Abraham's obedience to God. "How would you feel if I told you that God wants you to go to Africa right now, that you must leave your family and stay with a strange family? How do you think Abraham felt when God told him to leave everything and go into a strange land?"

4. Talk about our rewards. Have a happy mask and a sad mask. Explain that

whenever you obey God, he will reward you and you will be happy, but vice versa the other way. Ask the children, "Can you give me some examples of obeying God? Disobeying God? When you give me an example of obedience, I'll put up the happy mask, and when you give me an example of disobedience, the sad mask" (see Appendix).

5. *Abraham's test.*
   a. Direct a play including Isaac, Abraham, an angel, and a ram. Get costumes for the play (see Appendix).
   b. Do a puppet show or a shoe-box theater dramatizing Abraham, Isaac, and the angel (see Appendix).

6. Discuss Abraham's faith. Explain to the students how the test of Abraham is a proof of his extraordinary faith in God. God told him he would be the father of a great nation through his son Isaac. And even when God told Abraham to sacrifice Isaac, he still believed what God had promised to him. Abraham is called "our father in faith" because of this.

## Lesson Plan for a One-day Presentation

1. Pray.

2. Review chapter.

3. Illustrate "waiting" by doing activity 2.

4. Teach about Abraham's obedience and faith. See activities 3 and 6.

5. Show how important it is to obey. You may wish to do the activity suggested in activity 4.

6. Explain the test of Abraham. Assign readers for an in-class reading. Assign students to be the narrator, Abraham, and the angel.

## Suggested Schedule for a Five-day Presentation

1. Waiting for the Savior; Abraham
   *Aim:* to show God's tender care for his people who were waiting for the Savior; to identify Abraham as the father of God's people.
   *Activities:* see activities 2 and 3.

2. Plays, puppet shows
   *Aim:* to represent more vividly the story of Abraham's test.
   *Activities:* see activity 5a or 5b. Spend time in class making costumes, puppets, etc. See Activity Book for Chapter 5.

3. Plays, puppet shows
   *Aim:* to show God's tender care.
   *Activities:* see activity 5 or 6 and/or Activity Book for Chapter 5.

4. Our rewards
   *Aim:* to see the importance of obedience and to appreciate its reward.
   *Activities:* see activity 4.

5. Review
   *Aim:* to review this week's material.
   *Activities:* review game, quiz.

# CHAPTER 6

# The Prophet Moses

**Background Reading for the Teacher:**

Lawler, pp. 412−413.
Ex 1:1−13:22.

**Aims:**

The students should be able to identify the history of Moses and the Chosen People in Egypt; to review God's just punishments for those who disobey him; and to see and appreciate the role of God's Providence.

**Materials Needed:**

Blackboard, chalk, doll, basket, poster paper, cardboard, crayons, paints, sheets for costumes, etc.

## Activities

1. Complete the Activity Book assignment for Chapter 6.

2. Talk about God taking care of his people.
   a. Compare God to a mother caring for her newborn baby.
   b. Give a chalk talk.
   c. Make a "time line" of your life, showing how God is and has been carefully watching over you.

3. Talk about God's testing of us. "Why does God sometimes test us?" (See the second paragraph on page 27 of the students' text.) "What is the purpose of suffering? What are some tests God gives us?"

4. Have the students do some dramatizations, such as:
   a. Moses' being rescued (materials: doll, basket, costumes for Moses' mother and the Pharaoh's daughter).
   b. The burning bush. (Draw a likeness of a "burning bush" on cardboard or poster paper; have the voice of God come in from behind the bush.)

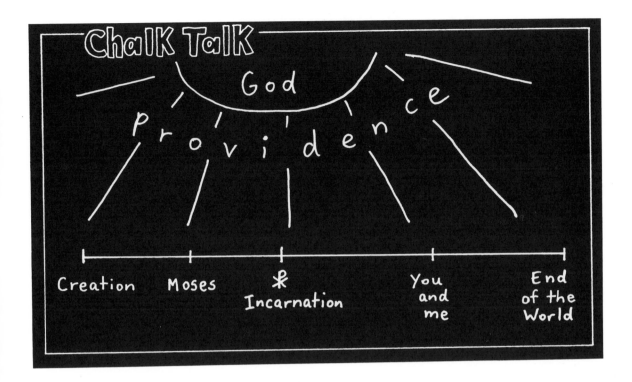

c. Moses and Pharaoh. (Get red paint and put in water to show the water turning into blood; have some toy "bugs" and let one student throw them on the floor to show another plague.)

d. Lamb's blood on the door. (Draw on the blackboard what it might have looked like.)

5. Make up a song of victory for the triumph of crossing the Red Sea.

**Lesson Plan for a One-day Presentation**

1. Pray.

2. Review.

3. Teach about God's special care for his Chosen People. Stress the truth that God watches over his people and blesses them as his own dear children.

Explain how the story of Moses is a perfect example of this loving care.

4. Give the chalk talk in activity 2b.

5. Teach about God's testing of his loved ones. Read aloud the paragraph on "testing" from the second paragraph of page 27.

6. Dramatize the chief incidents in Moses' life. For the sake of time, organize skits without the costumes and props.

**Suggested Schedule for a Five-day Presentation**

1. God's loving care for his people
   *Aim:* to understand and to appreciate how much God loves his people and watches over everything in their lives.

*Activities:* see activities 2a, 2b, and 2c. You may wish to hang up the students' time lines in your classroom.

2. The history of Moses and the Chosen People
   *Aim:* to identify the basic history of this important Old Testament narrative; to see the specific way God took care of his people.
   *Activities:* in-class reading of chapter 6. dramatizations (see activity 4; allow time for making props and costumes and rehearsing).

3. The history of Moses and the Chosen People
   *Aim:* see day 2.
   *Activities:* see day 2; present the dramatizations today.

4. The history of Moses
   *Aim:* to reinforce the history and the lessons contained in this history.
   *Activities:* see activity 5. Also, show filmstrip if one is available.

5. Review
   *Aim:* to review this week's material.
   *Activities:* review game, quiz.

**Notes:**

# CHAPTER 7

# King David

**Background Reading for the Teacher:**

Lawler, pp. 151–152, 462–463.
Hardon, p. 209.

**Aims:**

The students should be able to identify the two first kings, Saul and David; to see the specific kingly qualities of David; and to learn from David's example the value of trust in God and the importance of prayer.

**Materials Needed:**

Crayons, costumes, poster paper, blackboard.

## Activities

1. Dramatize an anointing. Use a holy water bottle or vase. Direct "Samuel" to pour water over the head of "David" (two students playing Samuel and David). Have Samuel put a crown on David's head (see Appendix).

2. Read the second paragraph on page 31 of the student text. Now draw pictures showing David's many great deeds.

3. Talk about David and Goliath. Ask: "Can you imagine yourself fighting an eighth-grader? Or how about someone in high school? This is what it might have been like for David to fight Goliath!" Tell them to:
   a. "Write down how you think David felt about fighting Goliath."
   b. "Now write down what prayer David might have said to overcome his fear."
   c. "Draw a picture of David and Goliath."

4. Talk about the Psalms. "Let us open our missalettes to the Psalm for today's Mass. Let us say this Psalm together. What are we saying?"

5. Make up a psalm of praise.

6. Tell the students that singing is "praying twice". Lead your children in a light, cheerful song, praising God.

7. *Prayer.*
   a. Give a chalk talk about how prayer equals talking to God.
   b. Ask for reports about the students' prayer charts.
   c. Compare prayer to talking with a friend . . . we are open with our friends, we tell them everything, good and bad. This talking with friends is like talking with God. We should be open to God, and tell him everything, good and bad.
   d. Make a visit to the Blessed Sacrament. Allow your third-graders a few minutes simply to talk to the Lord. Make sure they make reverent genuflections.

**Lesson Plan for a One-day Presentation**

1. Pray.

2. Review.

3. Tell the story of King David. Then do activity 3 in order to more vividly represent the story of Goliath.

4. Explain about the Psalms. Pass out missalettes and pray a Psalm for the upcoming week, preferably from a Sunday Mass.

5. Talk about prayer. See last paragraphs of the chapter and activities 7a and 7c.

**Suggested Schedule for a Five-day Presentation**

1. King David
   *Aim:* to identify the two first kings and especially to appreciate the kingly qualities in David.
   *Activities:* see activities 1, 2, and 3.

2. The Psalms
   *Aim:* to recognize and to appreciate the Psalms and any praise of God.
   *Activities:* see activities 4, 5, and 6.

3. King David and Jesus Christ
   *Aim:* to compare King David to Christ.
   *Activities:* Read the last paragraph in Chapter 7. How was David like Jesus? Draw a picture of King David and Christ the King.

4. Prayer
   *Aim:* to be familiar with prayer as a simple conversation with God.
   *Activities:* see activity 7.

5. Review
   *Aim:* to review this week's material.
   *Activities:* review game, quiz.

**Notes:**

# CHAPTER 8

# God's Laws of Love

**Background Reading for the Teacher:**

Lawler, pp. 275–277.
Hardon, pp. 288–295.

**Aims:**

The students should be able to review the doctrine of God's tender loving care and to identify and to appreciate the Ten Commandments as "God's laws of love".

**Materials Needed:**

Paper, hanger, poster paper, crayons, string, blackboard, chalk.

## Activities

1. Complete the Activity Book assignment for Chapter 8.

2. Review the teaching in Chapter 6 about God's loving care of his people. What specifically did God do to care for his people after they escaped Egypt? (See the first paragraph of this chapter, page 35).

3. Memorize the Ten Commandments.

4. On a large piece of poster paper, draw ten sections. Write one Commandment in each section and leave space for a cartoon. While you are teaching each Commandment, draw a cartoon in the space to illustrate a "do" and "don't" of each Commandment.

5. Make Commandment puzzles. Sketch on a piece of paper a "puzzle". Make sure the pieces fit together. (Be sure you have different shapes for each set.) You may wish to make three portions to a puzzle set. On each of the three portions, write down (a) a Commandment; (b) words of that Commandment, and (c) an example of living out that particular Commandment.

   Cut out the pieces. Direct the students to put them together.

6. Make a Commandment mobile. For this art project, you will need hangers, string, and paper (see the Appendix for more information). The aim is to reinforce the memorization of the Ten Commandments by making a mobile; each Commandment will hang from the wall, as a reminder to the students.

## Lesson Plan for a One-day Presentation

1. Pray.

2. Review (see activity 2).

3. Explain the Ten Commandments as "laws of love" that God, who desires only our holiness, gave us.

4. Direct your students in one of the suggested activities; especially recommended is the Commandment Mobile.

5. Assign Chapter 8 in the Activity Book as reinforcement or as homework.

**Notes:**

## Suggested Schedule for a Five-day Presentation

1. Review and introduction to the Ten Commandments
   *Aim:* to review the doctrine of God's loving care; to appreciate God's Commandments as "laws of love".
   *Activities:* see activities 1 and 2.

2. The Ten Commandments
   *Aim:* to memorize the Ten Commandments.
   *Activities:* see activities 1 and 4.

3. The Ten Commandments
   *Aim:* see day 2.
   *Activities:* see activity 5.

4. The Ten Commandments
   *Aim:* see day 2.
   *Activities:* see activity 6.

5. Review
   *Aim:* to review this week's material.
   *Activities:* review game, quiz.

# CHAPTER 9

# Loving God Most of All

**Background Reading for the Teacher:**

Lawler, pp. 296–297.
Hardon, pp. 296–313.

**Aims:**

The students should be able to explain the First Commandment, especially by stating why God alone deserves our adoration, identifying the "strange gods" that lead us away from him and showing the evil in superstitions. They should also be able to explain the Second Commandment, especially by stating why God demands reverence for his name and by stressing the power in the reverent saying of Jesus' name.

**Materials Needed:**

Blackboard, chalk, magazines, scissors for each student, poster paper, crayons.

## Activities

1. Complete the Activity Book assignment for Chapter 9.

2. Talk about adoration. Ask your students, "Can we ever love God too much?" Explain. List all the reasons why we adore God. (See first and second paragraphs on page 39 in the student text.)

3. Talk about "strange gods". Pass out magazines. Have students cut out pictures of "strange gods"—everyday persons, places, and things that can lead us away from God. (Have each student cut out a picture and prepare an explanation) "Why do the pictures you cut out seem to you to be strange gods?" Direct each student to come to the front of the room and explain why he chose his picture.

4. Tell the story of how St. Thomas Aquinas had a vision of God, a vision so beautiful that he regarded everything else on earth, even his own wonderful writings on God, as "straw". Ask the children , "Why did St.

Thomas think of such beautiful things, even his own very good descriptions of God, as just 'straw'?" Try to direct them to see how God is so much more than the best things on earth.

5. Ask your students if they know of any common superstitions. Have them tell why they are wrong. (N.b., do not mention any they have not heard of before.) (See Hardon, pp. 300–301.)

6. Discuss with your students how holy the name of Jesus is (see page 40 in the student text). Remind them that even the devils fear his name, and that is why we should say over and over, throughout the day: "Jesus". Introduce your students to the pious custom of bowing the head at the sacred name of Jesus.

7. Teach your third-graders the song "Father, I Adore You". Try to teach it to them as a round—the harmony when it is sung this way is beautiful.

8. Take your third-graders to make a visit to the Blessed Sacrament at your parish church or nearest chapel. Practice with them beforehand making reverent genuflections. In the church point out the various holy objects, such as the crucifix, altar, statues, relics, etc.

9. Develop your prayer charts (see Chapter 1, activity 9) by including prayers that are "quiet". Direct your third-graders to say spontaneous prayers during the day. Direct them to mark them on their prayer charts when they do so.

**Lesson Plan for a One-day Presentation**

1. Pray.

2. Review.

3. Explain about adoration and the First Commandment. See the first few paragraphs on page 39 of the text and activity 2.

4. Show your third-graders some pictures of "strange gods"; see activity 3. Explain what a strange god is and how careful we must be to adore only the true God.

5. Warn the children about superstitions; see activity 5.

6. End your lesson with an explanation about the holy name of Jesus (see text) and the value of saying his name over and over. See activity 6.

7. Assign Chapter 9 in the Activity Book as homework.

**Suggested Schedule for a Five-day Presentation**

1. Adoration
   *Aim:* to state why God alone deserves our adoration; to beware of "strange gods" by being able to identify them and to state the danger in them.
   *Activities:* see activities 2 and 3.

2. Adoration; the danger of superstition
   *Aim:* to grow in the appreciation of adoration for God; to identify the dangers of superstitions.
   *Activities:* see activities 3 (time for students to present their "gods" to the class), 4, 5, and 7 (take time to learn the song).

3. The holy name of Jesus
   *Aim:* to state why God demands reverence for his name; to show how powerful the name of Jesus is; to practice devotion to the name of Jesus.
   *Activities:* see activity 6. Sing the song "Father, I Adore You"; see activity 7.

4. Visit to the church; quiet prayers

   *Aim:* to learn the sacred objects in churches; to practice genuflecting reverently; to express spontaneous prayers to God; to realize the value of frequent, spontaneous prayers and aspirations.

   *Activities:* see activities 8, 9, and 1 (Activity Book). You may wish to sing "Father, I Adore You" in the chapel.

5. Review

   *Aim:* to review this week's material.

   *Activities:* review game, quiz.

**Notes:**

# CHAPTER 10

# The Lord's Day

---

**Background Reading for the Teacher:**

Lawler, pp. 415–420.
Hardon, pp. 313–316.

**Aims:**

The students should be able to state the reasons why we celebrate Sunday as the Lord's Day; to identify the Mass as the greatest act of worship; to identify and explain the holy days of obligation; and to list activities that help make Sunday a day of "joy and family closeness".

**Materials Needed:**

Poster paper, crayons, pictures of Jesus' rising from the dead, blackboard, chalk, hangers, strings, tape.

---

## Activities

1. Complete the Activity Book assignment for Chapter 10.

2. Talk about the meaning of Sunday. Instruct the children to draw pictures of "God resting" on the seventh day, Jesus' rising from the dead, and going to Mass. Remind them that these realities are the reasons why we celebrate Sunday as the Lord's Day.

3. Talk about Mass. Ask students: "What happens at Mass?" (See the third paragraph on page 43 of the text.)

4. Give a chalk talk.

5. Talk about the holy days of obligation.
   a. List and explain each holy day of obligation. Explain to the students why the Church allows us to celebrate the particular feast as a holy day. For example, we celebrate our Lady's Assumption into heaven because of Mary's importance in our salvation and because this feast reminds us of our future bodily resurrection into heaven.
   b. Instruct the children to draw pictures illustrating each holy day of obligation. For example, for August 15 they could draw Mary rising into heaven.
   c. The angels and saints celebrate with us on a special feast. Draw a picture of the "Celebration in heaven" that

goes on during a holy day of obligation.

6. Talk about Sunday, as a day of joy and family closeness.
   a. Read the last paragraphs in the chapter (in-class reading).
   b. Make up an "ideal" Sunday. List those activities God would want you to do. Make sure the children give you ideas on how to enjoy their Sunday with their families. Put their ideas on the blackboard.
   c. "What do you do on Sunday?" Be careful to guide the discussion away from personal, private affairs and on to ideas that might help the whole class.

7. Instruct your third graders to make a "holy-day mobile", in the same manner as you made the "Commandments mobile" (see the Appendix).

**Lesson Plan for a One-day Presentation**

1. Pray.

2. Review.

3. Instruct the children in the proper meaning of Sunday. Do the chalk talk in activity 4.

4. List and explain the holy days of obligation.

5. Describe an "ideal" Sunday.

6. End your lesson with giving the children time to draw. See activities 2, 5b, and 6c.

**Suggested Schedule for a Five-day Presentation**

1. Meaning of Sunday
   *Aim:* to state the reasons why we celebrate Sunday as the Lord's Day.
   *Activities:* see activities 2 and 3.

2. Holy days of obligation
   *Aim:* to identify and explain the holy days of obligation.
   *Activities:* see activity 5.

3. Holy days of obligation
   *Aim:* to reinforce the memorization of the holy days of obligation.
   *Activities:* see activity 8.

4. Sunday, the day of joy and family closeness
   *Aim* to list activities that help make Sunday a day of "joy and family closeness".
   *Activities:* see activity 6.

5. Review
   *Aim:* to review this week's material.
   *Activities:* see activity 1; quiz.

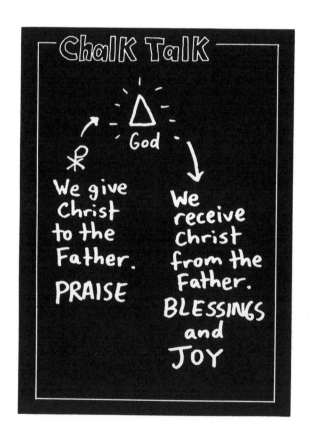

# CHAPTER 11

# Obedience and Love

**Background Reading for the Teacher:**

Lawler, pp. 333–334.
Hardon, pp. 317–350.

**Aims:**

The students should be able to state and explain the Fourth Commandment; to appreciate the role of parents; to identify the obedience in the early life of Christ; to see the Holy Family as the model family; to understand the virtue of obedience; to state and explain the Fourth Commandment; and to list ways to promote respect for life and respect for the poor and suffering.

**Materials Needed:**

Photos of the children's parents; pictures of the Holy Family; poster paper; paper; crayons; play microphone; shoe box; popsicle sticks; construction paper; costumes for the Child Jesus, St. Joseph, and Mary (see Appendix).

## Activities

1. See Activity Book assignment for Chapter 11.

2. Direct the children to get pictures of "your parents loving you" (for example, scenes of holding them as infants, feeding them, looking on them with love and pride, etc.). "Describe to the class what your parents are doing." This exercise is aimed at directing the children to think of their parents, God's representatives, with love.

3. Direct the students to make a "time line" of their parents' care for them. It may be wise for you to draw an example on the board.

4. Instruct the children to draw pictures of Jesus and St. Joseph, or Jesus and Mary, or the Holy Family. If possible, show them pictures of the Holy Family first. You may wish to read first the section on the Holy Family; see the fourth and fifth paragraphs on page 47 in the

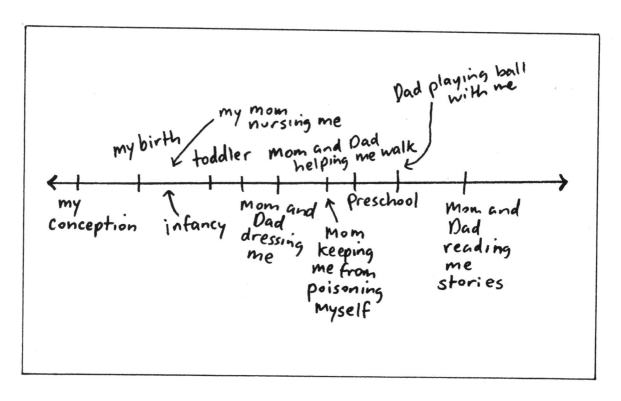

text. Stress the obedience of Jesus to Mary and Joseph as an example for each of us.

5. Conduct an "interview" with St. Joseph and Jesus. Appoint one third-grader to be St. Joseph, and another student to be Jesus. Ask simple questions, such as: "St. Joseph, how did Jesus listen to you?" "Jesus, did you ever talk back?" Make up a "microphone" with an orange-juice can and piece of rope tied, pasted, or taped to the inside of the can.

6. Make up a puppet show or shoe-box theater on the Holy Family (see Appendix).

7. Direct your pupils to make a list of all the sacrifices they can make to obey.

8. Add "Sacrifices" to the prayer chart. Direct your students to make a column entitled "Sacrifices". Every time they make a sacrifice, remind them to check it off and then show you at the end of the week.

9. Show pictures of the suffering who need our help. Emphasize to the students that our love should extend to all people of every age, race, color, and creed. Write on the board the words: Jesus said: "Whatever you do to the least of these brothers of mine, you do to me." Then erase the words *least of these brothers of mine* and *me*: "Whatever

you do to the _____ you do to _____."
Have the students fill in the blank with: poor, homeless, unborn, elderly etc. and the last blank with JESUS.

Have the students act out the story of the Last Judgment in Mt. 25:31–46, in which we are judged on the basis of charity. Let one of the boys be the king and the rest of the class divide into the good and the bad. The king judges and then the good ask: "Lord, when did we see you hungry. . . ."

10. Dramatize the story of the Good Samaritan. Use props and costumes.

11. Direct your students to make a list of all the ways they can respect life.

12. Make cartoons or draw stick figures of "Do's and don'ts" of the Fourth and Fifth Commandments.

## Lesson Plan for a One-day Presentation

1. Pray.

2. Review.

3. Explain about the duty we have to honor our parents. Draw a time line on the blackboard; see activity 3. Do an in-class reading on the description of Jesus as a child. List examples of obedience. Direct your children to write down ways they can obey their parents and teachers.

4. Tell the story of the Last Judgment.

5. Tell the story of the Good Samaritan. Explain about the importance of love for the suffering.

6. Go over with the students practical ways they can grow in their respect for the least of our brethren and all life. Be sure to stress the virtue of kindness.

7. End with the Activity Book assignment.

## Suggested Schedule for a Five-day Presentation

1. Honoring our parents
   *Aim:* to state and explain the Fourth Commandment; to grow in the appreciation of parents.
   *Activities:* see activities 2 and 3.

2. The Holy Family
   *Aim:* to identify the obedience in the early life of Christ; to see the Holy Family as the model family; to understand the virtue of obedience.
   *Activities:* see activities 4, 5, and 6.

3. The Fifth Commandment
   *Aim:* to state and explain the Fifth Commandment, what charity means, to love the "least" of our brothers and sisters, and to promote respect for all human life, and for all races.
   *Activities:* see activities 7, 8, and 9.

4. List of ways to put Fifth Commandment into practice
   *Aim:* to give practical suggestions
   *Activities:* see activities 10 and 11. Continue any unfinished activities above (8–9).

5. Review
   *Aim:* to review this week's material.
   *Activities:* see activity 12; review game, quiz.

# CHAPTER 12

# Purity and Truth

**Background Reading for the Teacher:**

Lawler, pp. 311–324.
Hardon, pp. 351–417.

**Aims:**

The students should be able to state and explain the Sixth, Seventh, and Eighth Commandments and the correlating Ninth and Tenth Commandments; to identify specific examples of positive and negative practices of the Commandments; and to understand each Commandment as specifically God's "law of love".

**Materials Needed:**

Poster paper, construction paper, crayons, blackboard, chalk.

## Activities

1. Complete the Activity Book assignment for Chapter 12.

2. Direct the students to draw pictures showing how important the body is. For example, they could show pictures of children running, eating, seeing beautiful things, etc. Ask the children to go up to the front of the class and explain why they drew what they drew.

3. Direct the pupils to draw a picture after they read from their text, page 51, the second paragraph, beginning with: "Your body is holy because on the day of your Baptism the Holy Spirit came to live inside it."

4. Direct the children to make a chart of "good" and "bad". List each Commandment; then list "good" examples and "bad" examples.

| Commandment | Good | Bad |
|:-----------:|:----:|:---:|
| 1 | | |
| 2 | | |
| etc. | | |

Let the students choose whether they wish to draw or write.

5. Direct a play featuring the four children who smashed their neighbor's window (see text).

6. Draw a mouth on the blackboard. Ask: "Why did God create the tongue and the mouth? He created the tongue and mouth to say the truth."

7. Tell stories of other saints who suffered for the truth, such as St. Margaret Mary, St. Catherine of Siena, and St. Bernadette.

8. Discuss the evil of damaging the reputation of another; stress the sinfulness of gossip and the need to speak well of our neighbors.

**Lesson Plan for a One-day Presentation**

1. Pray.

2. Review.

3. Teach about the dignity of the body (see the first two paragraphs on page 51 of the text) and the need for purity.

4. Teach about the Sixth, Seventh, Tenth, and Eighth Commandments.

5. Instruct your third-graders in one of the drawing activities; see activities 2 and 3.

6. End your lesson with an Activity Book assignment.

**Notes:**

**Suggested Schedule for a Five-day Presentation**

1. Sixth and Ninth Commandments
   *Aim:* to state and explain the Sixth and Ninth Commandments; to identify specific examples of positive and negative practices.
   *Activities:* see activities 2, 3, and 4.

2. Sixth and Ninth Commandments; Seventh and Tenth Commandments
   *Aim:* to state and explain the Sixth, Ninth, Seventh, and Tenth Commandments.
   *Activities:* see activities 2 (finishing from day 1) and 5.

3. Eighth Commandment
   *Aim:* to state and explain the Eighth Commandment; to give specific examples.
   *Activities:* see activities 6, 7, and 8.

4. Saints who lived out the Sixth, Seventh, Eighth, Ninth, and Tenth Commandments
   *Aim:* to learn about saints who lived out these Commandments
   *Activities:* show filmstrips on saints who lived out these particular commandments, such as St. Cecilia or St. Thérèse.

5. Review
   *Aim:* to review this week's material.
   *Activities:* review game, quiz.

# CHAPTER 13

# God's Tender Mercy

---

**Background Reading for the Teacher:**

Lawler, pp. 480–494.
Hardon, pp. 481–500.

**Aims:**

The students should be able to understand our God is all-loving, the Good Shepherd in search of his sheep; to identify Gospel stories on forgiveness; to show where and with what words Christ began the sacrament of penance; and to compare the forgiveness of a friend to the forgiveness of God.

**Materials Needed:**

Costumes (see Appendix), blackboard, chalk, poster paper, construction paper, crayons, pictures of shepherds, bottle.

---

**Activities**

1. Complete the assignment in the Activity Book for Chapter 13.

2. Make up a play about the shepherd who loves his sheep. See the description in the text. It might be helpful to have costumes, including sheep ears and "wool". Have one shepherd and a few children as sheep; direct them to "BAA!" Instruct one of the sheep to get lost and have the shepherd look for his poor lost sheep. Then talk about Jesus as the Good Shepherd.

3. Do some research on shepherds. Bring some simple pictures to class showing the work of shepherds. This will help the children understand why Jesus called himself the "Good Shepherd".

4. Direct the children to draw pictures of "Jesus, the Good Shepherd".

5. After describing to the children the great joy in heaven over one sinner who repents, suggest that they draw a picture of the kind of celebration the saints and angels might have in heaven (title it "Celebration in Heaven").

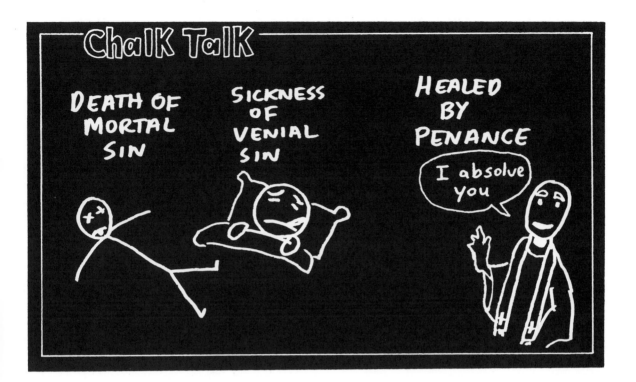

6. Make up a play on the story of Mary Magdalen and the pouring of precious oil on the feet of Jesus.

7. Direct your third-graders to memorize the Bible quote listed in the text: "Receive the Holy Spirit; if you forgive men's sins they are forgiven." Explain the importance of this quote, since it shows to us that Jesus really did want his priests to absolve our sins. If you want to make it easier, put it into a simple tune and sing it over and over with them.

8. Give a chalk talk (see the last paragraph of the text).

9. Talk about "Mary, Refuge of sinners", namely, how Mary flies to the sinner in order to help that person. Direct your children to draw a picture of Mary, Refuge of Sinners.

10. Make up a puppet show on shepherds and sheep by using brown paper bags, coloring them in.

**Lesson Plan for a One-day Presentation**

1. Pray.

2. Review.

3. Describe the work of shepherds. Put on a puppet show about shepherds; see activity 10.

4. Stress how much Jesus wants to forgive. Tell the story of Mary Magdalen. You may wish to act it out if you have time.

5. Help the students memorize the Bible quote on the institution of the sacrament of penance. You may wish to sing for them and encourage them to sing in order to memorize.

6. Explain about how Christ acts through the priest. Do the chalk talk as explained in activity 8.

7. Direct your children to draw pictures, as suggested in the activities above, and also to complete the Activity Book assignment.

**Suggested Schedule for a Five-day Presentation**

1. The Good Shepherd
   *Aim:* to understand our God is all-loving, the Good Shepherd in search of his sheep.
   *Activities:* see activities 2, 3, 4, and 10.

2. Jesus' love for sinners
   *Aim:* to identify Gospel stories on forgiveness.
   *Activities:* see activities 5 and 6.

3. Christ's acting through his priests
   *Aim:* to show where and with what words Christ began the sacrament of reconciliation.
   *Activities:* see activities 8 and 7.

**Notes:**

4. Reinforcement activity
   *Aim:* to reinforce the truth that Christ acts through his priests.
   *Activities:* Tell students about the absolute secret (or seal) of the confessional which priests keep. The priest will never tell anybody what you said. Tell the story of St. John Nepomucen. It is said that the king of Bohemia wanted to know what the queen said in the confessional. St. John Nepomucen refused to tell the king, so he was thrown into the river. He died rather than break the seal of the confessional. Ask a priest that the children know to come in and to explain what it is like to hear confessions. Usually, encounters of this kind with priests help to lessen the fear of going to confession.

5. Review
   *Aim:* to review this week's material.
   *Activities:* review game, quiz.

# CHAPTER 14

# Meeting Jesus in Confession

**Background Reading for the Teacher:**

Lawler, pp. 480–494.
Hardon, pp. 481–500.

**Aims:**

The students should be able to compare the sacrament of confession to the healing of a friendship; to explain the five steps of a good confession; to say with understanding the Act of Contrition prayer; and to state what contrition is and what is meant by an examination of conscience.

**Materials Needed:**

Poster paper, crayons, missalettes, blackboard, chalk, costumes, crucifix, construction paper.

**Activities**

1. Complete the assignment in the Activity Book for Chapter 14.

2. Do an in-class reading of the first paragraph. Then make up a skit about two friends who have a fight and then "make up". Compare the "making up" to the sacrament of confession.

3. Do a mnemonic diagram of the explanation in the text of "go to him, tell him we're sorry, resolve not to do it again, accept his forgiveness . . . " See chalk talk A.

4. Give chalk talk B, telling the "Story of a good confession". You can do the following either on the blackboard or on a roll of poster paper. If you do it on a roll of paper, you may wish to unroll it step by step. (Anyone can do stick figures!)

5. When explaining about sorrow, direct your students to look at a crucifix. "Just look at the crucifix. How much Jesus loved you . . . he died for you and your sins. . . . How can we ever think of hurting someone who loves us so much?"

Mnemonics (chalk talk A):

After looking at the crucifix, your children may write a prayer to express their sorrow.

6. Direct your third-graders to memorize the Act of Contrition listed in their texts. Make sure you go over each part of the prayer so it is not just a mechanical memorization. You may wish to make a puzzle out of construction paper with the words and illustrations of each phrase of the Act of Contrition. Your students can put the pieces together. In this way they will associate the words of the prayer with a picture.

7. Mnemonic on the questions at the end of this chapter.

*"How many things are required to make a good confession?"*

EASY AS PIE!

1. E   Ea   *Examine your conscience.*
2. S   s   *Sorrow for sin*
3. I   $\bar{e}(y)$   *Intention of not committing sin again*
4. A   as   *Accusation of our sin*
5. P   pie   *Penance*

8. Prepare a communal penance service. Usually the monthly missalettes contain them, especially missalettes in the months of December or February and March (the penitential seasons). Ask the priest to give a special homily for your third-graders.

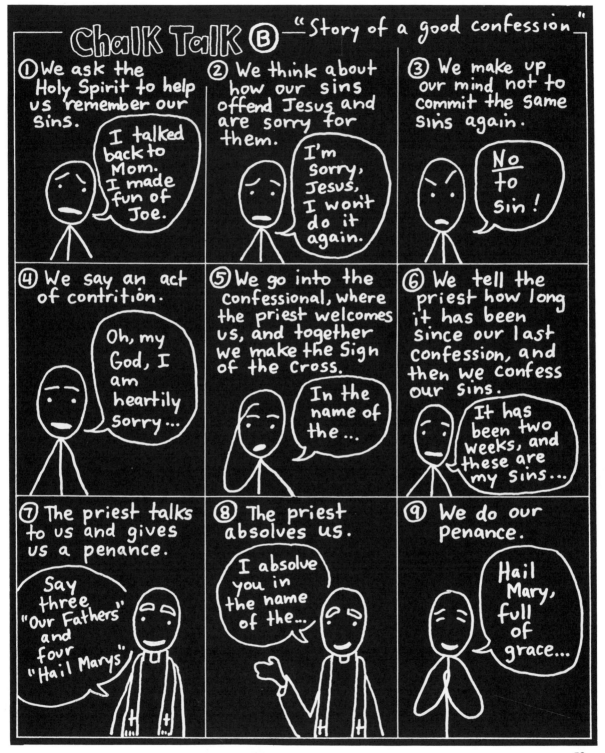

**Lesson Plan for a One-day Presentation**

1. Pray.

2. Review.

3. Teach about confession in terms of friendship; see activity 2.

4. Explain about the five steps to a good confession. You may wish to expand it into the nine steps, as exemplified in activity 4.

5. Make sure your third-graders know the Act of Contrition and also can explain what the phrases mean; see activity 6.

6. Complete the Activity Book assignment.

**Suggested Schedule for a Five-day Presentation**

1. Reconciliation, the restoring of a friendship
   *Aim:* to compare the sacrament of penance to the healing of a friendship.
   *Activities:* see activities 2 and 3.

2. Steps of a good confession
   *Aim:* to explain the five steps of a good confession.
   *Activities:* see activities 7 and 4.

3. The Act of Contrition
   *Aim:* to say with understanding the Act of Contrition.
   *Activities:* see activities 6 and 5.

4. Communal prayer service
   *Aim:* to participate in a communal prayer service.
   *Activities:* see activity 8.

5. Review
   *Aim:* to review this week's material.
   *Activities:* review game, quiz.

**Notes:**

54

# CHAPTER 15

# The Christ Child Is Born

---

**Background Reading for the Teacher:**

Lawler, pp. 93–123.
Hardon, pp. 156–160.

**Aims:**

The students should be able to appreciate the coming of Christ; to explain the story of the Annunciation and appreciate Mary's humility and obedience; to relate the chief points of the Christmas story; and to appreciate the spiritual lessons of Christmas.

**Materials Needed:**

Christmas music sheets, costumes for plays, Christmas recordings/tapes; record player or tape recorder, video, VCR, filmstrip and projector (optional).

---

**Activities**

1. Complete the assignment in the Activity Book for Chapter 15.

2. Ask the children to keep absolute silence for three minutes. Turn off all the lights. Wait for three minutes in silence. Then ask a student to turn on the light as you turn on a recording of some joyful Christmas music. Then ask, "How is this situation a little like the birth of Christ?"

3. Ask the students "What is a little baby like?" "Why did God become a little baby?" It would be even more vivid if you asked one of the mothers to bring in the younger baby brother or sister of one of your third-graders. Try to show them how amazing it is that God became a little infant.

4. Have an in-class reading of the story of the Annunciation. This is a very important lesson. Show the students the beauty of Mary's Yes to God. You may wish to pass around beautiful artistic portrayals of Mary's Yes. Point out Mary's bowed head, her hands together in prayer, showing her holiness.

## Chalk Talk

**Full of grace**

All grace. No sin.

**Not full of grace (all of us)**

Sins

tendency to sin

5. Dramatize the Annunciation. Choose a Gabriel, Mary, and a narrator. Add costumes for effectiveness.

6. Give a chalk talk on the Immaculate Conception.

7. After you teach the story of the Annunciation, it might be well to direct the children in prayer. "Let us think about saying Yes to God, as Mary did. Just think what beautiful events happened because Mary said Yes to God. Jesus came into our world. Let us remember that whenever we say Yes to God, great things can happen—for us and all around us. What are those things we must learn to say Yes to? Obeying quickly, speaking charitably, doing our chores and homework, saying our prayers? Let us pray quietly to God for a few minutes." After about two minutes say: "Now let us say a Hail Mary and ask Mary to help us. Hail Mary, full of grace . . . "

8. Dramatize the story of the Nativity. You may wish to use the text to do so. Once again, use costumes for greater effectiveness.

9. Lead the class in singing Christmas carols.

10. Ask, "What do you think of when you think of Christmas? Why?" Try to direct the students to relate the true practice of Christmas to imitating Jesus in his sacrifices.

11. This lesson may very well be in the Christmas season. If it is, it would be most fruitful for you to direct a full-fledged play. You may wish to present the play to the parents and your pastor.

12. Show a video or filmstrip related to the Christmas message. Some suggested ti-

tles for children of primary ages are:
*The City That Forgot Christmas* (VHS),
*I Will Take You to the Christ Child*
(VHS), and *The Night before Christmas
and Silent Night* (VHS).

### Lesson Plan for a One-day Presentation

1. Pray.

2. Review.

3. Make your children aware of the beauty
   and importance of the Annunciation,
   by reading the text and dramatizing the
   scene.

4. Lead your students in prayer, as is suggested in activity 7.

5. Explain about the spiritual importance
   of the Nativity, after you read the text.

6. If it is the Christmas season, lead them
   in Christmas carols. If it is not, you may
   wish to sing a Marian hymn or "We
   Three Kings".

7. Assign the exercise in the Activity
   Book for Chapter 15.

### Notes:

### Suggested Schedule for a Five-day Presentation

1. The Incarnation
   *Aim:* to make more vivid and more per-
   sonal the reality of the Incarnation.
   *Activities:* see activities 2 and 3.

2. The Annunciation
   *Aim:* to explain the story of the Annunciation and to appreciate Mary's humility and obedience.
   *Activities:* see activities 4, 5, 6, and 7.

3. The Nativity
   *Aim:* to relate the chief points of the
   Christmas story.
   *Activities:* see activities 8, 9, and 10.

4. Reinforcement Activities
   *Aim:* to reinforce the spiritual meaning
   of Christmas.
   *Activities:* see activities 11 or 12.

5. Christmas Play and Review
   *Aim:* to present the play and to review
   this week's material.
   *Activities:* review game, quiz.

# CHAPTER 16

# Jesus Grows in Age and Wisdom

**Background Reading for the Teacher:**

Lawler, pp. 81–97.
Hardon, pp. 141–144.

**Aims:**

The students should be able to identify the specific virtues Jesus practiced in the hidden life and how they can practice them in their own lives; to identify Jesus' baptism and more deeply appreciate their own baptism; to appreciate the first announcements that Jesus is the Savior and how his public life began.

**Materials Needed:**

Blackboard, chalk, poster paper, costumes, filmstrip or video, projector, missalettes, Bibles.

## Activities

1. Complete the assignment in the Activity Book for Chapter 16.

2. Ask your students, "What for you is an 'ordinary day'? Write down on a piece of paper what you do in an ordinary day. Now, what things do you do that you think Jesus also did? What ordinary things do we see Jesus doing in the Gospel?"
   a. Conduct a discussion on how we can imitate the virtues of Jesus. Keep the discussion based on what the Gospel says.
   b. Direct your third-graders to write down the virtues they wish to practice. Suggest that they add these virtues to the prayer and sacrifice chart.

3. a. Give a chalk talk on "hidden life".
   b. Make a list of all the "hidden things" you can do for God. See page 71 in the text. Tell how in the Gospels Jesus disapproves of those who "show

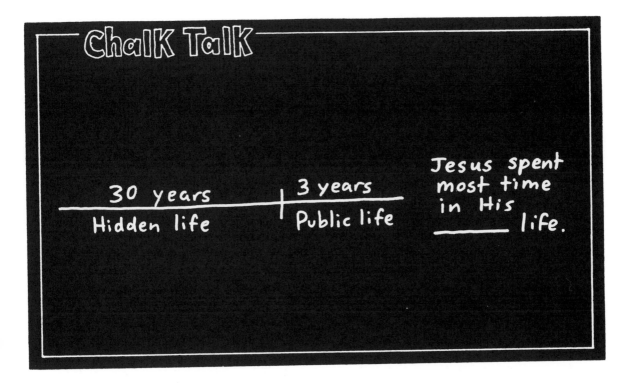

**Chalk Talk**

30 years
Hidden life

3 years
Public life

Jesus spent most time in His _____ life.

off" when they do something. (e.g., Mt. 6:1–6, 16–18; 23:5–72). Encourage your pupils to do "hidden things" for God alone.

4. Tell the children more about John the Baptist. Have a class discussion. "What did he tell the people to do?" (be sorry for their sins) "How can we prepare for Jesus?" (by being sorry for our sins) "What did John the Baptist announce?" (the Promised One) "Who is the Promised One?" Other names: Savior, Messiah, Redeemer, Son of God. Jesus. "When was he promised? Why was he promised?" "How did John announce the Promised One?" (See Luke 3:16.) Tell the story of John the Baptist pointing to Jesus and announcing: "Behold the Lamb of God, who takes away the sin of the world" (John 1:29). "What did he mean by these words?" (He was announcing that Jesus was the Savior who would save the people from their sins. He would sacrifice himself like a lamb. He would die for us.) Ask if any of the students have ever heard these words before. (The priest says them at Mass.) Dramatize John the Baptist (optional) or have students quiz each other.

5. a. Explain the baptism of Christ. "What did the voice of God the Father say?" Make sure that students understand that God identified Jesus as his Son, the Second Person of the Holy Trinity. The Holy Spirit came down, etc.

   b. Relate it to their own baptism.

6. Teach your children a song in the missalettes that is commonly sung, such as "Follow Christ", "Take My Hands", or "Spirit of God". Go over the words

with your students so they will sing with their hearts as well as their voices.

## Lesson Plan for a One-day Presentation

1. Pray.

2. Review.

3. Teach what is meant by an "ordinary life". Compare the ordinary life of Christ to the ordinary lives of third-graders in your class; see activity 2.

4. Explain the virtue of Jesus in his hidden life and how the students can do similar acts of virtue; see activities 2 and 3.

5. Go over Jesus' baptism.

6. End with a song; see activity 6.

7. Assign homework in the Activity Book.

## Suggested Schedule for a Five-day Presentation

1. Jesus' hidden life
   *Aim:* to identify the ordinary life of Christ with the students' own lives.
   *Activities:* see activities 2 and 3.

2. The virtues of Jesus' hidden life
   *Aim:* to identify the specific virtues Jesus practiced in the hidden life.
   *Activities:* see activities 2 and 3.

3. Announcing the mission of Jesus
   *Aim:* to understand John the Baptist and what and whom he is announcing in order better to understand the mission of Jesus.
   *Activities:* see activity 4.

4. Jesus' Baptism
   *Aim:* to identify the baptism of Jesus and to help students more deeply appreciate their own baptism.
   *Activities:* see activity 5.

5. Review
   *Aim:* to review this week's material.
   *Activities:* see activity 6; review game, quiz.

**Notes:**

# CHAPTER 17

# Signs and Wonders

**Background Reading for the Teacher:**

Lawler, pp. 112–125.
Hardon, pp. 108–113, 122–124.
Fulton J. Sheen, *Life of Christ*.

**Aims:**

The students should be able to identify the beginning of Jesus' public life; to know and explain some of his miracles and why he performed them; to know some of the parables and what they mean; to express some of the holy and beautiful virtues of Jesus and why people were so deeply attracted by him.

**Materials Needed:**

Missalettes, watercolors, water, jars, video, tape of *The Greatest Story Ever Told*, filmstrip and projector, construction paper, poster paper, crayons, play microphone, Bibles.

## Activities

1. Complete the Activity Book assignment for Chapter 17.

2. Describe why Jesus Christ attracted so many people. Explain how so many people came from all over just to see and hear him. Using a play microphone, have your pupils pretend to be those people in Galilee. Interview the "people" and ask what they think about Jesus.

3. Teach your children to sing a song related to this lesson. Look in your missalettes for an appropriate song, such as "Those Who Know Christ", "Follow Christ", "We Are the Light of the World", etc.

4. a. Tell the story of or direct a play on "The Miracle at Cana" (Jn 2:1–10). Tell the students why Jesus performed this miracle. (out of love for the couple and to honor their marriage)

   b. Explain or dramatize the "miracles of loaves".

5. Dramatize the story of the Roman centurion. Have your "centurion" don a sword (see Appendix).

6. Dramatize other miracles of Christ, or at least tell some of them: the ten lepers (Lk 17:11–19), the two blind men (Mt 9:27–30), the raising of the dead boy (Lk 7:11–17).

7. For the section on the raising of Lazarus, you may wish to show the famous scene from *The Greatest Story Ever Told,* in which Lazarus rises from the dead to the tune of Handel's *Messiah.* The scene is good for showing the astonished expressions on the faces of the people. Tell the students more about the story of Lazarus (Jn 11:1–44). Ask, "Why was it such a great miracle?" If necessary, remind the students that (a) Lazarus had been buried for four days, and his body was already decaying; (b) Christ revealed who he was: "I am the Resurrection and the Life . . . " and Martha said: "I have come to believe that you are the Messiah, the Son of God: he who is to come into the world." (Jn 11:27); (c) a big crowd was waiting and watching as if to say: "We think he cannot do anything now."

8. After explaining about parables, have some guessing games:
   Tell them more about the parable "The Sower and the Seed" (Mt 13:4–9). Then have them guess the meaning. Help them with the answers (see Mt 13:18–23).
   Guess what the mustard seed means (Mt 13:31–32).
   Tell them more parables:
   The Pearl of Great Price (Mt 13:45–46). Guess what it means? (God and his kingdom are more valuable and precious than anything else in our lives, and should be put first.)

The Wheat and the Weeds (Mt 13:24–30). Guess what it means? (Mt 13:36–43)
   Make sure they can relate these parables to their own lives.

9. Draw pictures of a miracle, talk, or any other scene in the life of Jesus.

10. Do a chalk talk in which you discuss the difference between being proud and being humble.

11. Read this to your third-graders, and direct them to fill in the rest on a sheet of paper: I am an enemy of Jesus when I . . . I am a friend of Jesus when I . . .

**Lesson Plan for a One-day Presentation**

1. Pray.

2. Review.

3. Talk about why Jesus attracted so many. Describe how the crowds came from all over to see him. Have an in-class reading of the first paragraph of the chapter.

4. Describe the miracles of Jesus (see the text). You may wish to do one of the plays (see the activities).

5. Teach about parables and do activity 8.

6. End with encouragement to be humble and a warning of the danger of pride; see activities 10 and 11.

7. Assign homework in the Activity Book.

**Suggested Schedule for a Five-day Presentation**

1. Why Jesus attracted so many.
   *Aim:* to express some of the attractive qualities of Jesus Christ.
   *Activities:* see activities 2 and 3.

2. The miracles
   *Aim:* to list and explain some of his miracles.
   *Activities:* see activities 4, 5, 6, and 7.

3. The miracles of Christ
   *Aim:* to appreciate the wonder in the miracles.
   *Activities:* see activities 4, 5, 6, and 7.

4. Parables; pride versus humility
   *Aim:* to explain about parables and to see the importance of humility.
   *Activities:* see activities 8, 9, 10, and 11.

5. Review
   *Aim:* to review this week's material.
   *Activities:* review game, quiz.

**Notes:**

# CHAPTER 18

# The Last Supper, Our First Mass

---

**Background Reading for the Teacher:**

Lawler, pp. 409–447.
Hardon, pp. 457–458.

**Aims:**

The students should be able to connect the Last Supper with the feast of Passover; to identify the specific wishes of Jesus at the Last Supper; to appreciate his Great Commandment to love one another and to serve others with humility; to identify his words at the Last Supper with the words during the Consecration; and to appreciate more the Mass as a reliving of the Last Supper.

**Materials Needed:**

Pictures of the Last Supper, construction paper, crayons, missalettes or songbooks, basin, water, towels.

---

**Activities**

1. Complete the exercise in the Activity Book for Chapter 18.

2. Ask your students, "Think of someone you love very much. Now imagine that this person is about to die. He is on his deathbed and asks you, 'Will you do something in my memory? Will you say a Hail Mary for me every day, so I will soon get to heaven?' How many of you would do this small act? How many would not? This is like the apostles and Jesus at the Last Supper. Jesus was about to die, and, just before he died, he asked his friends to 'do this in remembrance of me'."

3. Show a picture of the Last Supper. Point out Jesus, St. John, Judas, the way they were seated, the bread and wine, etc.

4. Direct your students to draw a picture of the Last Supper.

5. Tell the story of how Jesus taught his lesson of humility (see the top of page 81 in the text, "First Jesus gave them a lesson . . ."). Reenact the washing of the disciples' feet. Appoint a Jesus and the Twelve. Have a basin of water and towels. Remind the students how the apostles must have felt to have their leader wash their feet—the duty of a slave. Washing of the feet was something done by servants at the time of Jesus. The fact that the Lord Jesus, the Son of God, washed the feet of others shows us with what great love he humbly served us, and how willing we, his creatures, should be to serve each other with love. Let students give ways in which they can serve others. Show pictures of the Pope washing the feet of others. Tell how the Pope, the bishops, and priests serve us. Let the pupils give examples of ways in which they serve us.

6. Lead your children in the singing of the song "Do This in Memory of Me", which is found in most missalettes, or a similar song.

7. Direct your students to find the words of Consecration in their missalettes. Parallel these words to the words of the Last Supper (see the text).

8. Add "Going to Mass" to the prayer chart. Encourage your students to attend daily Mass, or at least to attend more than once a week.

9. Organize a class Mass. Practice with a lector; appoint a reader for the prayers of the faithful; direct four pupils to carry gifts. You may find it helpful to have your children write "sacrifices/resolves to love God more" on a piece of paper and then, during the time when the baskets are passed, have them place their "offering" to God in the basket. Thursday would be an ideal day for such a Mass.

**Lesson Plan for a One-day Presentation**

1. Pray.

2. Review.

3. Explain to your third-graders the Last Supper as the first Mass. Have an in-class reading of the description of the Last Supper. Point out various characters in pictures of the Last Supper.

4. Go over the Words of Consecration in the missalette. Remind the students of how reverent and quiet they should be at this sacred time.

5. Direct your pupils in the singing of a eucharistic song.

6. Ask your students to draw pictures of what they have studied, such as the Last Supper scene, the washing of the feet, or the Mass.

7. Assign the students homework in the Activity Book for this chapter.

**Suggested Schedule for a Five-day Presentation**

1. The Last Supper
   *Aim:* to identify the specific wishes of Jesus at the Last Supper; to connect the Last Supper with the feast of Passover.
   *Activities:* see activities 2, 3, and 4.

2. Jesus' Commandment to love
   *Aim:* to identify the specific wishes of Jesus at the Last Supper, namely, to love one another as he has loved us.
   *Activities:* see activity 5.

3. The Holy Mass
    *Aim:* to identify his words at the Last Supper with the words of Consecration.
    *Activities:* see activities 6, 7, 8, and 9.

4. The Holy Mass: a class Mass
    *Aim:* to appreciate more the Mass as a reliving of the Last Supper.
    *Activities:* see activity 9.

5. Review
    *Aim:* to review this week's material.
    *Activities:* review game, quiz.

**Notes:**

# CHAPTER 19

# Jesus Gives His Life for Us

**Background Reading for the Teacher:**

Lawler, pp. 125–137.

**Aims:**

The students should be able to describe Jesus' Passion; to identify ways to imitate Jesus in his sufferings; and to know how to make the Stations of the Cross.

**Materials Needed:**

Missalettes, pictures of Jesus in his sufferings, crucifix, "Stations of the Cross" booklets for children, construction paper, regular paper, crayons, filmstrip and projector.

## Activities

1. Complete the exercise in the Activity Book for Chapter 19.

2. Show pictures of Jesus' agony, after describing and reading about it. Ask the students to write down responses, such as "Jesus, I'm so sorry for having caused your agony . . . "

3. Tell the story of the Sacred Heart of Jesus and what Jesus said about people who ignore him. Ask your children, "How can you console the Heart of Jesus?" Emphasize that Jesus freely chose to suffer and die out of love for us.

4. Have an in-class reading from the text, beginning at: "Later in the night . . ." Comment to your students about Jesus' gentleness and silence in the midst of terrible suffering. Ask them to fill in: "I can be silent like Jesus when . . . "; "I can be gentle like Jesus when . . . "

5. Direct your third-graders to make up a simple chart called "Jesus and Me". Have them write down under "Jesus" a suffering of Jesus, then draw this (as in the agony or the scourging). Then, under "Me", have them write down what they as third-graders can do to imitate Jesus.

Example:

| Jesus | Me |
|---|---|
| Followed the soldiers | Obey my teachers |

In doing this exercise, be sure to point out how light our sufferings are in comparison with those of Jesus.

6. Show a picture of the crown of thorns. Or, better yet, make a crown of thorns so your children can see how large the thorns were and how much he must have suffered.

7. Talk about Jesus' forgiveness of his persecutors. Encourage your students to forgive everyone who has hurt them in any way.

8. Show a filmstrip or filmstrips on the Passion of Christ.

**Lesson Plan for a One-day Presentation**

1. Pray.

2. Review.

3. Explain about Jesus' sufferings by describing his agony, scourging, and crowning. Show pictures, if possible. Conduct an in-class reading.

4. Direct your children to make a chart comparing themselves to Jesus; see activity 4. Stress his virtues of gentleness, forgiveness, and courage.

5. Assign an exercise in the Activity Book.

**Suggested Schedule for a Five-day Presentation**

1. The agony in the garden
   *Aim:* to describe Jesus' agony and to console him in his sufferings.
   *Activities:* see activities 2, 3, and 8.

2. The carrying of the Cross, the crowning with thorns, and the death of Jesus
   *Aim:* to describe the Passion of Christ; to strive to imitate his virtues and to offer up small sacrifices.
   *Activities:* see activities 4, 5, 6, and 7.

3. Reinforcement activities
   *Aim:* to reinforce the lesson through visual means.
   *Activities:* see activity 8.

4. Stations of the Cross
   *Aim:* to make the Stations of the Cross.
   *Activities:* see the list of the Stations of the Cross in the text. Take your third-graders to church. Ask one student to carry a cross, and, using a children's Stations of the Cross booklet, lead your children in saying the Stations. Explain to them about obtaining a plenary indulgence. Encourage them also to sing. You may wish to appoint a student with a clear voice as a "prayer leader".

5. Review
   *Aim:* to review this week's material.
   *Activities:* review game, quiz.

# CHAPTER 20

# Offering Gifts of Love

---

**Background Reading for the Teacher:**

Lawler, pp. 409–419.
Hardon, pp. 457–458.

**Aims:**

The students should be able to explain and understand the meaning of "sacrifice"; to describe the history of sacrifice; to identify the "great goal" of all Old Testament sacrifices: reconciliation with God; and to see the sacrifice of Jesus as the perfect Sacrifice renewed in every Mass.

**Materials Needed:**

Missalettes, paper, crayons, filmstrip and projector, blackboard.

---

## Activities

1. Complete the exercise in the Activity Book for Chapter 20.

2. Point out to the children what a sacrifice is *not*. You may ask, "What is a 'sacrifice' in baseball? Is this what we mean when we speak of offering sacrifices to God? Of course not. We can best understand sacrifice by thinking about the sacrifices made by people who love someone. For example, what kind of sacrifices has your mother made for you? Is it always easy for your mother to get up to feed her baby? to change diapers? to clean up after her sick children? Why does she do these things?" (because she loves her children. She gives up something—her time, her sleep—in order to make them happy.) "Sacrifice is the way we express love for someone. So, when we sacrifice, we show God we _____ him."

3. Tell your children O. Henry's famous story *The Gift of the Magi*. Relate very simply how "a young husband and young wife, who were very poor, each wanted to buy something special for the other at Christmas. The young wife had beautiful long hair, so what do you

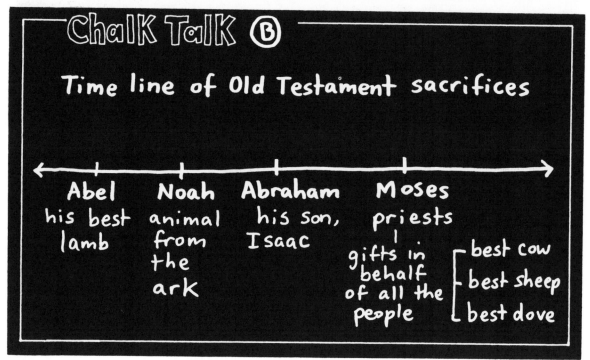

think she did? She cut it and sold it so she could buy her husband a watch case. Her husband, who knew about how much his wife loved her hair, pawned his precious watch and bought for his wife a beautiful comb. They sacrificed what was most previous to each of them because they _____ each other."

"What kinds of sacrifices can you do for God? To be a real sacrifice, a sacrifice should be something beautiful and something that we love very much. Then the sacrifice shows God how much we love him."

4. Give chalk talks A and B.

5. "The Mass is like a 'time machine'. What is a time machine? It is a machine that can take you back in time. How is the Mass like a time machine?"

6. Give chalk talk C on the continual offering of the Holy Mass.

7. As you explain about how Mass is the continual re-presentation of Calvary, (see text, last paragraph), you may wish to show the children pictures of Padre Pio, the famous stigmatic (explain what a stigmatic is) who would bleed profusely during his offering of Holy Mass.

8. As an art assignment, tell the students to draw a picture of them offering themselves to the Father with Jesus during Holy Mass.

9. Show a filmstrip related to this lesson.

10. Teach your third-graders a song relating to the theme of this lesson. See the missalettes for some suggestions.

11. Take time in class to make an act of self-

offering in union with all the Sacrifices of the Mass throughout the world.

**Lesson Plan for a One-day Presentation**

1. Pray.

2. Review.

3. Explain about sacrifice by pointing out what it is not and to what it can be compared; see activity 2. Conduct an in-class reading of the first few paragraphs of the text, explaining sacrifice.

4. Draw a "time line" of Old Testament sacrifices; see chalk talk B.

5. Teach about how Jesus is the perfect sacrifice; see chalk talk A.

6. Review the Mass as the continual re-presentation of Calvary.

7. Encourage the students to attend Mass and to offer to the Father the Masses now being offered all over the world.

8. End your lesson with the art assignment in activity 8.

9. For a homework assignment, have students complete the exercise in the Activity Book.

## Suggested Schedule for a Five-day Presentation

1. Sacrifice
   *Aim:* to explain and understand the meaning of sacrifice.
   *Activities:* see activities 2, 3, and 4. Also, ask the children what sacrifices they can make—today, this week, or this year.

2. Jesus, perfect Sacrifice offered continually in the Mass
   *Aim:* to identify the "great goal" of all Old Testament sacrifices, reconciliation with God; to see Jesus as the perfect Sacrifice; to appreciate the renewal of his Sacrifice in every Mass.
   *Activities:* see activities 4, 5, 6, 7, and 8.

3. Reinforcement activities
   *Aim:* to reinforce the understanding and appreciation of the Mass as Sacrifice.
   *Activities:* see activities 8, 9, 10, and 11.

4. Class Mass
   *Aim:* to foster reverence and understanding of the Mass through actual participation.
   *Activities:* see Chapter 18, activity 8 and 9.

5. Review
   *Aim:* to review this week's material.
   *Activities:* review game, quiz.

**Notes:**

# CHAPTER 21

# The Holy Mass

**Background Reading for the Teacher:**

Lawler, pp. 415–419.
Hardon, pp. 465–471.

**Aims:**

The students should be able to review the effects of Jesus' Sacrifice on the Cross; to appreciate the Mass as the perfect act of praise; and to identify and understand the particular sections of the Mass, namely, the Introductory Rite and the Liturgy of the Word.

**Materials Needed:**

Missalettes, costumes, paper, crayons, filmstrip and projector.

## Activities

1. Complete the exercise in the Activity Book for Chapter 21.

2. Direct your students to list the effects of the Sacrifice on the Cross (see first paragraph on page 93 in the text).

3. Stress the Mass as a miracle. Review examples of miracles. Ask your third-graders, "How is the Mass the greatest miracle?"

4. Ask your pupils to draw a picture of the priest offering the Eucharist in the name of Christ.

5. Ask a priest to come into your class to give a talk about the Mass, specifically, about the Consecration of the bread and wine into the Body and Blood of Christ.

6. After reading the section starting with "We go to Mass every Sunday . . ." (p. 93) ask your students to write a prayer to God, expressing what they are thinking about when they offer the Mass with the priest.

7. Hand out missalettes to each of your pupils. Explain to them that they will be

going through the parts of the Mass, step by step.

8. Begin with the Entrance Antiphon. Ask, "Why do we stand when the priest enters? What words of greeting does the priest give us?" Go over the idea of "greeting" and translate this notion into the holy greeting in the Introductory Rite of the Mass.

9. "What do we do at the very beginning of Mass?" (The answer is in the text, "At the beginning of the Mass, we . . . ") Go over with your third-graders the Sign of the Cross. Urge them to make it reverently. In fact, you should take time to have them make the Sign while you watch to see how reverent they are.

10. Go over the penitential rite. Review with them the idea of forgiveness and sorrow for our many sins. Talk with them about saying we are sorry to friends whom we love and the great importance of saying we are sorry to God.

11. Act out the Introductory Rite. Appoint a boy as a priest, with two altar boys, and someone carrying the Lectionary. Ask the class to be the congregation. Have an opening song.

12. Remind the students that when they say the *Gloria*, they are joining the angels in singing the praises of God. Direct them to draw a picture of angels praising God. Remind them that the angels are with them when they pray at Mass.

13. Explain to your third-graders that God speaks to them through the priest. Remind them to sit erect, with their eyes fixed on the priest, listening intently to what God is saying through him. Tell them not to look around, which would be being discourteous to God. Ask

them why we stand when the priest reads the Gospel.

14. Act out the Liturgy of the Word. Again, appoint a boy to play the part of the priest and ask him to give the congregation a "homily".

15. Explain why the Creed is so important.

16. Show a filmstrip.

17. Sing an appropriate hymn, such as "We Gather Together" or another fitting song.

**Lesson Plan for a One-day Presentation**

1. Pray.

2. Review.

3. Explain the Mass as a miracle. Show pictures, if possible, of the Mass.

4. Go over the Introductory Rite and the Liturgy of the Word, as suggested in activities 7–15.

5. End the lesson with drawing or singing.

6. Assign the completion of the Activity Book exercise for this chapter.

**Suggested Schedule for a Five-day Presentation**

1. The renewal of Jesus' Sacrifice in the Holy Mass
   *Aim:* to review the effects of Jesus' Sacrifice on the Cross; to appreciate the Mass as the perfect act of praise.
   *Activities:* see activities 2, 3, and 4.

2. The miracle of the Mass
   *Aim:* to appreciate the Mass as the perfect act of praise.
   *Activities:* see activities 4 and 5 (the visit of a priest and his explanation).

3. The introductory rite
   *Aim:* to appreciate and understand the introductory rite of the Mass.
   *Activities:* see activities 7, 8, 9, 10, 11, and 12.

4. The Liturgy of the Word
   *Aim:* to appreciate and to understand the Liturgy of the Word.
   *Activities:* see activities 13, 14, and 15.

5. Reinforcement activity
   *Aim:* to reinforce what has been learned about the Mass.
   *Activities:* see activities 16 and 17.

6. Review
   *Aim:* to review this week's material.
   *Activities:* review game, quiz.

**Notes:**

# CHAPTER 22

# Offering Jesus to the Father

**Background Reading for the Teacher:**

Lawler, pp. 419–429.
Hardon, pp. 458–465, 471–481.

**Aims:**

The students should be able to identify, explain, and appreciate the Liturgy of the Eucharist; and to explain and express reverence for the Real Presence of Jesus.

**Materials Needed:**

Paper, crayons, pictures of the miracle of Lanciano, bells, missalettes, a paten, filmstrip and projector.

**Activities**

1. Complete the exercise in the Activity Book for Chapter 22.

2. Talk about gifts. Ask your third-graders, "What was the last gift you received that you really liked? What was the last gift that you gave that really made you happy to give? Why is gift giving a joy? Why do we like to give gifts to people we love? Why, then, should we love to give gifts to God?"

3. Direct your students to read quietly the section on bread and wine. Then ask, "What is meant by bread and wine?"

4. Remind the children about the presence of the angels at Mass. Show them pictures of angels hovering at the altar. Read them sayings from the saints about angels at holy Mass. Urge them to pray to their guardian angels before Mass so that their angels will help them be attentive.

5. Remind them that the angels sing, "Holy, Holy, Holy . . . " Direct them to draw pictures of angels singing "Hosanna" and the people joining the angels.

6. Bring a bell to class. Ring the bell and tell them that in some Masses today, and in all Masses in the past, a bell would be rung during the Consecration to remind the people that Christ was renewing his Sacrifice and that the bread and wine were now the Body, Blood, Soul, and Divinity of Jesus Christ.

7. Describe the kinds of posture and prayerful positions the children should have during the Consecration. Tell them this is the most sacred time. Urge them to bow their heads respectfully.

8. Ask your students what they would do if you told them Jesus was next door. Compare the presence of Jesus when he lived on earth to the Presence of Jesus at the Consecration. How thrilled we should be that he is truly there.

9. Have the students write a prayer describing their love toward Jesus in the Sacred Host and Precious Blood.

10. Show the students a paten. Tell them how Jesus is truly present in every particle of the Sacred Host and how the paten is designed to catch any particle.

11. Discuss how to be reverent during Consecration. Suggest to them ways to practice external reverence, if they need these suggestions.

12. Show a filmstrip on the Eucharist.

13. Sing the eucharistic hymn.

14. Throughout this lesson, use the missalettes and point out the sections in the Liturgy of the Eucharist.

**Lesson Plan for a One-day Presentation**

1. Pray.

2. Review.

3. Explain to the students about the Mass as a gift to the Father; see activity 2.

4. Go over the Liturgy of the Eucharist with the missalettes, using some of the ideas given in the activities.

5. Explain how Jesus is present Body, Blood, Soul, and Divinity in every particle of the Host. Show a paten and explain its use; see activity 10.

6. Urge the students toward deep reverence. Take them to the church to make a visit.

7. You may wish to end with a song or a drawing activity.

8. Assign as homework the exercise in the Activity Book.

**Suggested Schedule for a Five-day Presentation**

1. Gifts; Liturgy of the Eucharist
   *Aim:* to appreciate the Mass as the perfect gift to the Father; to identify the parts in the Liturgy of the Eucharist.
   *Activities:* see activities 2, 3, 4, and 5.

2. Liturgy of the Eucharist
   *Aim:* to identify, understand, and appreciate the Liturgy of the Eucharist.
   *Activities:* see activities 6, 7, and 8.

3. Liturgy of the Eucharist
   *Aim:* to express reverence toward Jesus' Presence in the Consecration.
   *Activities:* see activities 9, 10, 11, and 13.

4. Reinforcement Activities
   *Aim:* to reinforce the lessons learned.
   *Activities:* filmstrip and/or visit to the Blessed Sacrament.

5. Review
   *Aim:* to review this week's material.
   *Activities:* review game, quiz.

# CHAPTER 23

# The Bread of Life

**Background Reading for the Teacher:**

Lawler, pp. 421–424.
Hardon, pp. 465–471.

**Aims:**

The students should be able to explain how the Sacrifice of the Mass forms a bond between heaven and earth; to explain why Jesus is the Lamb of God; and to identify the Eucharist as our spiritual food and Sacred Banquet uniting us in Christ.

**Materials Needed:**

Missalettes, blackboard, filmstrip and projector, paper and crayons, pictures of lambs.

## Activities

1. Complete the exercise in the Activity Book for Chapter 23.

2. Talk about Jesus as the Lamb of God. Tell the students about lambs, namely, their response before butchering—whereas a goat will kick and fight, a lamb will go calmly to its death. "Why is Jesus called the Lamb of God? Who pointed to Jesus and said, 'Behold the lamb of God'?" (John the Baptist)

3. Show pictures of lambs. Ask your students to draw pictures of lambs and tell how the lambs remind them of Jesus.

4. Have the students fill in:
   I am like a goat when . . .;
   I am like a lamb when . . .

5. Have an in-class reading beginning with the third paragraph on page 103. Have your third-graders open their missalettes to the Communion Liturgy and find "This is the Lamb of God who . . ." Remind them of what they should say and do, namely, kneel reverently and say, "Lord, I am not worthy to receive you . . ."

6. Ask the students, "Why are we not worthy to receive Jesus?" Tell the stu-

dents the story of the Roman centurion, from whom the Church gets the words, "Lord, I am not worthy . . . " (Mt 8:5–13).

7. The Eucharist is food that nourishes us. "What does food do? How does the Eucharist do the same for our souls?" (We need it for the life of our souls.) "What does it give us?" (It pours love into our souls, Jesus, who is love. It gives us grace to love others.) "What does it do to us?" (It unites us in a bond of love with Jesus and all others of every nation and race.) All who partake in the Eucharist are united in one body. Other names for the Eucharist are Bread of Life, Bread of Angels, and Bread of Heaven.

8. Sing a simple Communion song.

9. Tell the story of St. Clare, "who was very sick and was missing Christmas Mass. She so very much wanted to go to Mass, but she had to stay in her little room. (St. Clare was a nun.) God gave her a miracle. From her room, which was separate from the chapel, she was able to see the Mass. How? Her room was not near the chapel. A miracle! This shows how pleased Jesus is with our holy desires. Do we have holy desires? Do we want to go to Mass and receive Communion?"

10. Show a filmstrip on Communion or saints who loved to receive Communion.

**Lesson Plan for a One-day Presentation**

1. Pray.

2. Review.

3. Explain how Jesus is the Lamb of God. Have an in-class reading of the first two paragraphs of the chapter.

4. Describe the effects from receiving Holy Communion.

5. Discuss the Eucharist, the Bread of Life. Teach a eucharistic song; spend some time singing.

6. Assign the exercise in the Activity Book.

**Suggested Schedule for a Five-day Presentation**

1. Jesus, the Lamb of God
   *Aim:* to explain why Jesus is the Lamb of God.
   *Activities:* see activities 3 and 4.

2. Communion rite
   *Aim:* to identify and understand the Communion rite.
   *Activities:* see activities 5 and 6.

3. Appreciation of Communion
   *Aim:* to appreciate Communion.
   *Activities:* see activities 7, 8, and 9.

4. Reinforcement activity
   *Aim:* to reinforce the lessons in this text.
   *Activities:* see activity 10.

5. Review
   *Aim:* to review this week's material.
   *Activities:* review game, quiz.

# CHAPTER 24

# Jesus Comes to Us
# In the Holy Eucharist

---

**Background Reading for the Teacher:**

Lawler, pp. 419–421, 428–429.
Hardon, pp. 471–481.

**Aims:**

The students should be able to identify the Eucharist as the Bread of Life; to explain the three things necessary to receive our Divine Guest; to understand what is meant by a thanksgiving after Communion; and to appreciate the beauty and privilege in receiving Jesus in Communion.

**Materials Needed:**

Missalettes, blackboard, filmstrip and projector, paper and crayons, costumes for a play on St. Tarcisius.

---

**Activities**

1. Complete the exercise in the Activity Book for Chapter 24.

2. Compare preparing for Jesus as a guest in our hearts to preparing for earthly guests. Ask, "What does your mother do when you are expecting a special guest? For example, what would your mother do if the Pope would come to your house this evening? Would she make sure the house was in order? Would she have out her best silver-ware? Would she make a special dinner? Why? How is this preparation for a special guest the kind of preparation we should make for Jesus? Preparing well for someone means we really care about him and want him to feel respected and loved."

3. Use a mnemonics device to help the students remember. "Remember: B, G, F! B, G, F! *B*elieve, be in *G*race, and *F*ast are the three things necessary for

receiving Jesus." Explain each of the three.

4. Say: "What should you do after Holy Communion? Why? Jesus is truly present, and we should pay attention to him. If someone were talking to you, and you looked around and talked to other people, we would say you were rude. Jesus is truly present with us in Holy Communion. You must not talk to others; pay attention to Jesus and tell him how much you love him."

5. Have the students write a prayer of thanksgiving to Jesus and pretend that they just received him.

6. Give a chalk talk.

7. Ask: "Whom" do you most like to be with? Describe your friend. Why do you like to be with him or her? Now, why should we want to be with Jesus?

By receiving Communion devoutly (devoutly means paying attention to Jesus), we get very close to Jesus and can enjoy his company. He becomes, as he really is, our very best friend."

8. *St. Tarcisius.*
   a. Tell the story of St. Tarcisius (see the text, p. 108).
   b. Show the filmstrip on St. Tarcisius, if one is available to you.
   c. Put on a play on "St. Tarcisius". This story is perfect for third-graders. Choose a Tarcisius, a Pope, a soldier, and pagan boys. Wad up papers for rocks. Use old sheets and curtains for costumes; see Appendix for swords, beards, and so on.

9. Say every day and teach your third-graders to sing "O Sacrament Most Holy, O Sacrament Divine, All Praise

and All Thanksgiving Be Every Moment Thine".

10. As an art assignment, tell the students: "Draw a picture of yourself receiving Communion. Write down a prayer underneath. Hang the picture up in your bedroom, if it is all right with your mother."

11. Direct the students to find "Communion Rite" in their missalettes.

## Lesson Plan for a One-day Presentation

1. Pray.

2. Review.

3. Explain the importance of preparation for Communion; see activity 2.

4. Describe how one should make a thanksgiving; see activities 3 and 4.

5. Tell the story of St. Tarcisius.

6. End with the song "O Sacrament Most Holy . . . "

7. Assign the exercise in the Activity Book.

## Suggested Schedule for a Five-day Presentation

1. Preparing for our Divine Guest
   *Aim:* to explain and to appreciate why we should prepare to receive Jesus in Communion.
   *Activities:* see activities 2 and 3.

2. Communion thanksgiving
   *Aim:* to understand what is meant by a thanksgiving after Communion.
   *Activities:* see activities 4 and 5.

3. Our love for frequent Communion
   *Aim:* to appreciate the beauty and privilege in receiving Jesus in Communion.
   *Activities:* see activities 6, 7, 9, and 11.

4. St. Tarcisius
   *Aim:* to follow the example of St. Tarcisius, who died defending the Eucharist; to imitate his great love for the eucharistic Jesus.
   *Activities:* see activity 8.

5. St. Tarcisius
   *Aim:* to present a short play about St. Tarcisius.
   *Activities:* see activity 8b. You may wish to invite other classes, parents, and/or your pastor to see the children perform.

**Notes:**

# CHAPTER 25

# Jesus Rises in Splendor

**Background Reading for the Teacher:**

Lawler, pp. 137−149.
Hardon, pp. 38, 145−146.

**Aims:**

The students should be able to describe the scene of the Resurrection; to state that suffering and death will be turned into glory and everlasting life; to describe the forty days before the Ascension; and to explain why we can be full of joy and hope knowing Jesus is King of heaven and earth.

**Materials Needed:**

Costumes for plays, missalettes, paper and crayons, blackboard, filmstrip and projector.

## Activities

1. Complete the exercise in the Activity Book for Chapter 25.

2. Divide the class into groups and assign them different scenes or tell the following in dramatic story form:
   a. Early Easter Sunday: the women, the angel, and the apostles (see the first two paragraphs on page 111 in the text). Make costumes for the women and angels; use perfume bottles for spices and oils; make a "big stone" (Mt 28:1−10; Mk 16:1−9; Lk 24:1−8).
   b. Mary Magdalen and Jesus (Jn 20: 11−13).
   c. Jesus appearing in the Upper Room (Lk 24: 36−43).
   d. Jesus appearing to Thomas (Jn 20:24−29).
   Throughout these plays it might be helpful to have soft but joyful music playing to provide more atmosphere.

3. a. Teach the children to sing glorious Easter hymns; one suggestion might be the popular "Jesus Christ Is Risen Today".

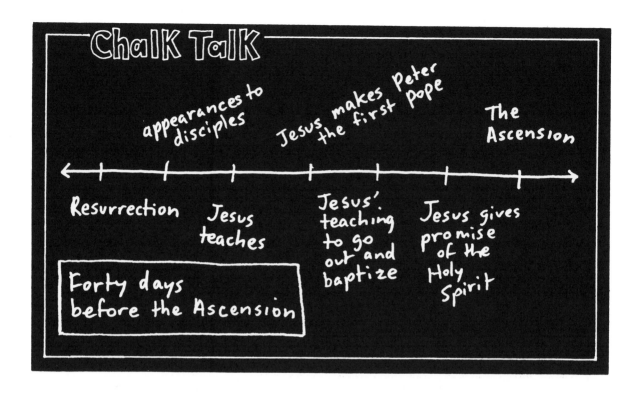

b. Say the prayers at the end of the chapter.

4. Direct your third-graders to make up a chart showing how suffering turns into glory. You might give some examples and put them on the board.

| Every suffering turns into | glory. |
|---|---|
| My sufferings | My glory |
| Being made fun of | Reward in Heaven |
| Being sick | Suffering with Christ |
| Being scolded by mistake | Gaining grace |

5. As a chalk talk or an art project, make a time line for the forty days before the Ascension.

6. Show pictures of Jesus' Ascension into heaven. Read the quote at the end of the chapter (Mt 28:19–20).

7. Ask, "What must it have been like to be with Jesus during those forty days?" Direct the students to draw pictures of being with Jesus. Remind them he still had and still has his five wounds. They should draw the wounds into the picture of Jesus.

8. Draw a picture of Jesus, King of heaven and earth.

9. Show a filmstrip on the glorious mysteries of the holy Rosary.

**Lesson Plan for a One-day Presentation**

1. Pray.

2. Review.

3. Tell in story form (dramatize your voice and expressions as much as possible) the Easter scenes.

4. Explain how all of our sufferings, like the sufferings of Jesus, will turn into glory; see activity 4.

5. Describe Jesus' stay on earth for forty days. Draw a time line.

6. Ask the students to draw pictures with their crayons of the Easter scenes and the Ascension scenes. Tell them you will hang up their pictures.

7. Make a visit to the church. Point out the Paschal candle.

8. Assign for homework the exercise in the Activity Book for this chapter.

**Suggested Schedule for a Five-day Presentation**

1. Easter Sunday
   *Aim:* to describe the Resurrection scene and the other visits from the Risen Lord; to state that suffering and death will be turned into glory and everlasting life.

*Activities:* see activities 3 and 4. Also, you may wish to take your third-graders into the church to see first-hand the Paschal candle described in the text.

2. Forty days before the Ascension and the Ascension
   *Aim:* to describe the forty days before the Ascension, and the Ascension; to explain why we can be full of joy and hope knowing Jesus is King of heaven and earth.
   *Activities:* see activities 5, 6, 7, and 8.

3. Filmstrip on the first two glorious mysteries
   *Aim:* to reinforce through visual means the lessons of this week.
   *Activities:* see activity 9; show only the first two mysteries.

4. Play preparation day
   *Aim:* to reinforce through dramatization the Gospel scenes.
   *Activities:* see activity 2.

5. Play presentations
   *Aim:* to present the plays worked on the day before.
   *Activities:* presenting the plays to an audience, such as another class, parents, priests, etc.

**Notes:**

# CHAPTER 26

# The Coming of the Holy Spirit

> **Background Reading for the Teacher:**
>
> Lawler, pp. 150–161.
> Hardon, pp, 185–186, 214–215.
>
> **Aims:**
>
> The students should be able to describe the descent of the Holy Spirit; and to identify and explain the fruits of the Holy Spirit.
>
> **Materials Needed:**
>
> Paper and crayons, filmstrip and projector, costumes, pictures of the descent of the Holy Spirit, pictures of beautiful temples, Catholic periodicals with pictures.

## Activities

1. Complete the exercise in the Activity Book for Chapter 26.

2. Act out the descent of the Holy Spirit as it is described in the text. It would be helpful to appoint a few students to produce "sound effects" (the strong wind). You will need a girl for Mary, a few boys for the apostles. You may tell the story in dramatic story form instead. (See Acts 2:1–5.)

3. Show your third-graders pictures of the descent of the Holy Spirit. Ask them to draw pictures of what they thought it was like.

4. Show pictures of beautiful temples (such as the Taj Mahal). Explain that each one of us is more beautiful than the most beautiful temple: we are temples of the Holy Spirit.

5. Lead your children in a prayer to the Holy Spirit.

6. Go over the fruits of the Holy Spirit (page 117 in the text). Describe each fruit. Ask the students to memorize these fruits.

7. Tell a story or stories of saints. Ask your children if they can see the fruits of the Holy Spirit in the saints.

8. Sing the well-known song "Come, Holy Ghost", which is on page 119 in your text.

9. Have your third-graders cut out pictures from Catholic periodicals of "the fruits of the Holy Spirit alive in others" (such as pictures of Mother Teresa, for charity; someone stopping a fight, for peace; a teacher, for patience!).

## Lesson Plan for a One-day Presentation

1. Pray.

2. Review.

3. Tell, in dramatic story form, the events surrounding the descent of the Holy Spirit (see your text).

4. Remind the students that the Holy Spirit is in every soul in the state of grace. Go over the fruits of the Holy Spirit and give examples of saints whose lives showed these fruits.

5. Have your children draw pictures of the descent of the Holy Spirit.

6. End your class by teaching the students a song to the Holy Spirit, such as "Come, Holy Ghost".

7. Assign for homework the completion of the exercise in the Activity Book.

**Notes:**

## Suggested Schedule for a Five-day Presentation

1. Descent of the Holy Spirit
   *Aim:* to describe the descent of the Holy Spirit.
   *Activities:* see activities 2 and 3.

2. Temples of the Holy Spirit
   *Aim:* to identify the person in grace as a temple of the Holy Spirit.
   *Activities:* see activities 4 and 5.

3. Fruits of the Holy Spirit
   *Aim:* to identify and explain the gifts of the Holy Spirit.
   *Activities:* see activities 6, 7, and 9.

4. Filmstrip on the descent of the Holy Spirit
   *Aim:* to reinforce the lesson through audiovisual means.
   *Activities:* show a filmstrip on the Holy Spirit.

5. Review
   *Aim:* to review this week's material.
   *Activities:* review game, quiz.

# CHAPTER 27

# God's Family on Earth

**Background Reading for the Teacher:**

Lawler, pp. 174–222.
Hardon, pp. 219–240.

**Aims:**

The students should be able to identify Peter as the first Pope; to state the duties of the Pope, the bishops, priests, religious, and the laity; and to see how we are all united in one family, the family of the Catholic Church.

**Materials Needed:**

Blackboard, paper and crayons, picture of the Pope, Catholic periodicals with pictures, filmstrip and projector, costumes for play.

## Activities

1. Complete the exercise in the Activity Book for Chapter 27.

2. Show a picture of the Pope. Explain how he is the successor of St. Peter.

3. Direct a play in which the students act out the bestowal of Peter's office as Pope (see text). Have costumes, and maybe some graphic signs, such as a rock, keys, or binding tape.

4. Direct your students to cut out pictures of the Pope from recent Catholic periodicals. They could make either a montage or collage of their collected photos.

5. Give chalk talk A on the different roles in the Church.

6. Make a puzzle out of the following terms: Pope, Vicar of Christ; bishop, the Shepherd; priests, bishops' helpers, who forgive sins and offer Mass; religious, those called to give everything to God in a special way; laity, the baptized, believing members of God's family who are to make the world holy. Students could design puzzles for each other.

7. Show a filmstrip on a saint who showed how someone loved God with his whole heart and soul.

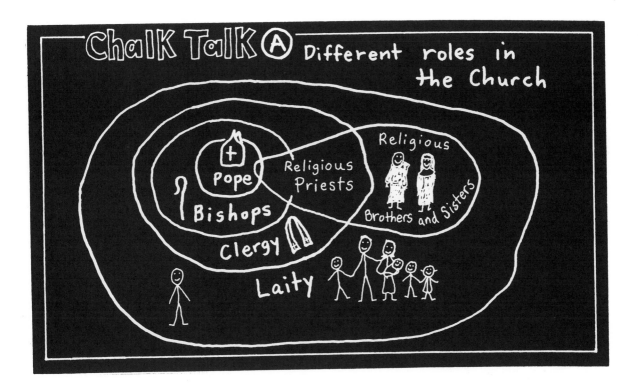

**Chalk Talk Ⓐ Different roles in the Church**

Pope

Religious Priests

Religious Brothers and Sisters

Bishops

Clergy

Laity

8. For chalk talk B, draw a picture of a body on the board. Explain how we are all united in one body under Christ.

9. Ask the students when was the last time they were all together in a family celebration, such as Thanksgiving, Easter, etc. What was it like? Explain how we are all one big family in the Church.

10. Suggest that everyone offer a prayer or sacrifice for the Church, knowing the Church is our family. Ask them how one sin can hurt the entire Church.

11. Tell the students about St. Thérèse, who offered up little sacrifices for the Church. One day she was working very hard, and she was sick. When asked to stop working so hard, she explained, "I must work and offer up my sufferings for missionaries." When we are sick or tired or find school hard, we should also offer up our pains for the _____.

**Lesson Plan for a One-day Presentation**

1. Pray.

2. Review.

3. Tell the students the story of how Jesus gave St. Peter the power to be the first Pope. Dramatize this story by bringing in a rock, keys, and binding tape. Remind them of the Pope's power to teach the truth.

4. Show the interrelation among the Pope, bishops, priests, religious, and laity through chalk talk A.

5. Remind the students that we are all called to be saints and to help our family the Church. Tell them the story of a

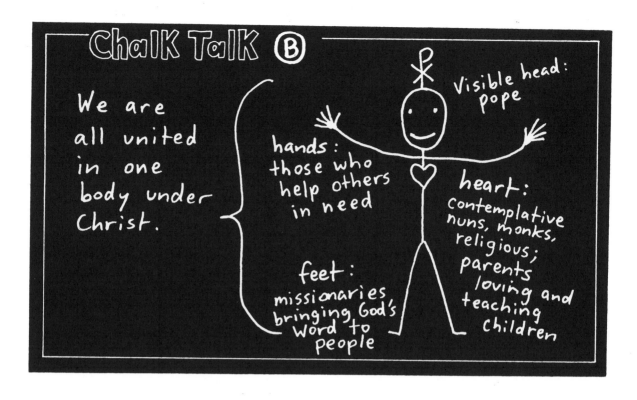

saint who lived out the call to holiness, such as St. Thérèse or St. Dominic Savio or the little children of Fatima.

6. Direct the students to draw a picture of "Our Family, the Catholic Church" in any way they want, showing what they have learned during this lesson.

7. Assign the exercise in the Activity Book for this chapter.

**Suggested Schedule for a Five-day Presentation**

1. Peter, the first Pope
   *Aim:* to identify Peter as the first Pope.
   *Activities:* see activities 2, 3, and 4.

2. Different roles in the Church
   *Aim:* to state the different roles and their different duties.
   *Activities:* see activities 5 and 6.

3. Call to holiness
   *Aim:* to identify how a saint lived out his or her call to holiness and try to imitate the saint's good example.
   *Activities:* see activity 7.

4. Unity in one body
   *Aim:* to see how we are all united in one family, the family of the Catholic Church.
   *Activities:* see activities 8, 9, 10, and 11.

5. Review
   *Aim:* to review this week's material.
   *Activities:* review game, quiz.

# CHAPTER 28

# Our Life in the Church

---

**Background Reading for the Teacher:**

Lawler, pp. 253–262.
Hardon, pp. 505–510.

**Aims:**

The students should be able to identify and explain the meaning of signs; to explain how a sacrament is a sign; to list the sacraments and point to their signs; and to make a list of intentions for which to pray.

**Materials Needed:**

Blackboard, paper and crayons, periodicals (Catholic), scissors, paste, costumes and props for plays.

---

## Activities

1. Complete the exercise in the Activity Book for Chapter 28.

2. Dramatize different signs, such as yawning to signify sleepiness or boredom, jumping up and down to signify excitement, or crying to signify sadness. Act out a sign and then let your third-graders guess what it is.

3. Reverse roles, and have your students make up signs for the others to guess.

4. For each of the sacraments, bring out "props" to point to their sacramental signs. For example:

Baptism: water and the gesture and words the priest uses.

Eucharist: bread and wine (it might be helpful to get some unconsecrated hosts).

Penance: say the words and raise your hands as a priest would; you might show the stole the priest wears for this sacrament (the stole, though not a sign of this sacrament, does show the priest's power).

Holy Orders: stole.

Matrimony: picture of a bride and groom giving the sacrament to each other.

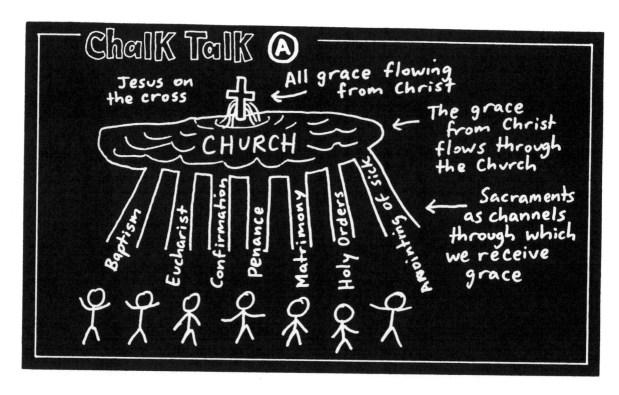

Confirmation: holy oil, words.

Sacrament of the Sick: holy oil, holy water, etc.

5. Give chalk talk A on the Church as the reservoir of grace.

6. Give chalk talk B on "Baptism and the Life of Grace".

7. Direct your students to make a booklet on "The Sacraments". Have them color and sketch a sign or symbol for each of the sacraments or cut out pictures which remind them of the sacraments.

8. Have a prayer service. Ask your pupils, after you read the last section of the text on prayer, for whom they should pray. Remind them how much Jesus wants all to be saved. Tell them that our Lady of Fatima asked that we pray much for poor sinners. Then ask them, "For whom shall we pray?" After you write their intentions on the board, spend some time praying. You may wish to say a decade of the Rosary, or have a class Mass in which the priest offers his Mass for the children's intentions.

**Lesson Plan for a One-day Presentation**

1. Pray.

2. Review.

3. Explain about signs, giving apt examples and even dramatizing, as explained in activities 2 and 3.

4. Point to the sacraments as signs. Use props, if possible, or draw signs on the board. Ask the students to draw and color the seven sacraments' signs.

5. Talk about the life of grace; see chalk talk in activity 6.

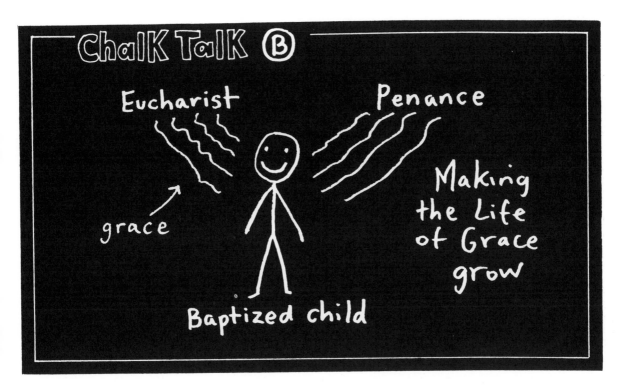

**Chalk Talk Ⓑ**

Eucharist

Penance

grace

Making the Life of Grace grow

Baptized child

---

6. Remind the students about the important duty of praying for all, especially those who do not know God. End your class with a little time for prayer for these people.

7. Assign the exercise in the Activity Book for homework.

**Suggested Schedule for a Five-day Presentation**

1. The meaning of signs.
   *Aim:* to identify and explain the meaning of signs.
   *Activities:* see activities 2 and 3.

2. The signs of the sacraments
   *Aim:* to explain how a sacrament is a sign; to list the sacraments and to point to their signs.
   *Activities:* see activity 4.

3. The signs of the sacraments
   *Aim:* to list the sacraments and to point to their signs.
   *Activities:* see activity 7.

4. Baptism and the life of grace; prayer for those who do not know God
   *Aim:* to see how baptism brings us grace, and how we must nurture this life of grace; to learn the importance of prayer for all.
   *Activities:* see activities 5, 6 and 8.

5. Review
   *Aim:* to review this week's material.
   *Activities:* review game, quiz.

# CHAPTER 29

# Mary, Our Mother and Queen

**Background Reading for the Teacher:**

Lawler, pp. 97–112.
Hardon, pp. 150–172.
John J. Delaney, *A Woman Clothed with the Sun* (Doubleday and Co., Inc., 1960).

**Aims:**

The students should be able to identify Mary as the Mother of the Church; to describe the life of Mary; to express external devotion to Mary; and to list ways to imitate Mary.

**Materials Needed:**

Paper, crayons, blackboard, filmstrip and projector, pictures of Mary, crown for a May crowning, pictures of our Lady of Guadalupe and our Lady of Fatima.

## Activities

1. Complete the exercise in the Activity Book for Chapter 29.

2. Draw a picture of Jesus on the Cross giving Mary to us.

3. Draw a chart on the board, or direct your students to make one, illustrating saying Yes or No to God.

| What God asks of me | Yes | No |
|---|---|---|
| take out trash | obedience | disobedience |
| Cheer up someone who is sad | obedience | disobedience |

4. Mention that Mary was not only born, but also conceived, without sin.

5. Pray daily, "O Mary conceived without sin, pray for us who have recourse to thee."

6. Show a filmstrip on one of the Marian apparitions (such as Fatima, Guadalupe, or Lourdes). Mention Mary's message of prayer and obedience to God's laws.

7. Ask the students: "What is easier, to go to your mother or to your father when you have done something wrong or you want something?" (Usually, but not always, it is easier to go to your mother.) Compare this natural human relationship with the kind of relationship we should have with Mary our Mother, who goes to Jesus for us.

8. Direct the students to write a personal prayer to Mary, expressing their admiration to her and asking her for favors.

9. Direct the students to describe a typical day in their life. Suggest that they ask themselves throughout each activity they describe, "What would Mary do? How would she act?"

10. Have a bulletin board display or a chalk talk on Mary, our Queen and our Mother.

11. Conduct a crowning of Mary. Have a large statue and make a crown out of artificial or real flowers; see May missalettes for some suggestions for hymns. A good time to crown Mary would be during this unit, on May 1, or on a Marian feast day.

12. Ask, "Who is your favorite lady? Why? What do you like in her? How is Mary the perfect woman?" (All the good qualities in women we know are only a shadow of what Mary is like.)

**Lesson Plan for a One-day Presentation**

1. Pray.

2. Review.

3. Explain why Mary is Mother of the Church. Review Marian doctrines (see text).

4. Compare Mary to an earthly mother. Suggest ways to imitate Mary.

5. Tell stories (dramatize as much as possible) about Marian apparitions. Children love to hear about these, and you are teaching such valuable lessons.

6. End with a prayer and song to Mary.

7. Assign the Activity Book exercise for Chapter 29.

**Suggested Schedule for a Five-day Presentation**

1. Mary, Mother of the Church
   *Aim:* to identify Mary as Mother of the Church.
   *Activities:* see activities 2, 3, 7, and 10.

2. The Life of Mary
   *Aim:* to describe the life of Mary.
   *Activities:* see activities 4 and 5.

3. Marian apparitions
   *Aim:* to identify Mary's apparitions and to understand her messages.
   *Activities:* see activity 6; also, have an in-class reading of the section on our Lady of Guadalupe (p. 117).

4. Imitation of Mary/devotion to Mary
   *Aim:* to imitate Mary.
   *Activities:* see activities 3, 8, 9, 11, and 12.

5. Review
   *Aim:* to review this week's material.
   *Activities:* review game, quiz.

# CHAPTER 30

# The Communion of Saints

**Background Reading for the Teacher:**

Lawler, pp. 511–543.
Hardon, pp. 254–278.

**Aims:**

The students should be able to state the real meaning of death, the doorway to heaven; to see the most important goal of life: loving God and others so as to enter heaven; to identify and describe heaven, Purgatory, and hell; and to identify the Communion of Saints and the Last Judgment.

**Materials Needed:**

Paper and crayons, blackboard, filmstrip and projector, book on saints, songbook.

## Activities

1. Complete the exercise in the Activity Book for Chapter 30.

2. Have students draw pictures of what they think heaven will be like. (Have an in-class reading of the first paragraph of the chapter.)

3. Give chalk talk A.

4. Tell stories of great saints who showed their love for God in ways a third-grader can appreciate, for example: St. Thérèse of Lisieux, St. Dominic Savio, St. Maria Goretti, the little children of Fatima, and St. John Bosco.

5. Urge your children to pray for the holy souls in Purgatory. Your may wish to teach them the prayer "May the souls of the faithful departed, through the mercy of God, rest in peace, *Amen.*"

6. Have a class Mass. Appoint lectors, servers, etc. Ask the priest to offer the Mass for the holy souls in Purgatory. You may wish to have your third-graders bring a quarter each to collect money for a stipend. Carefully explain the nature of a stipend, that is, we do not buy prayers!

7. Give chalk talk B.

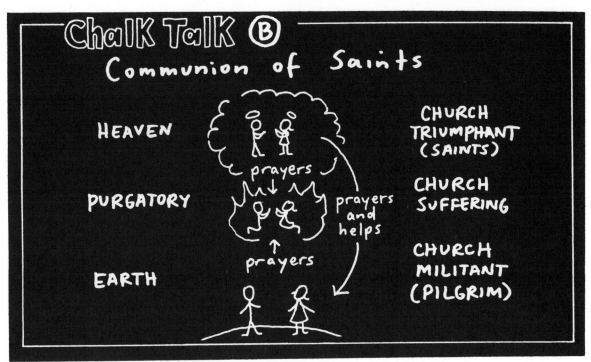

8. Ask the students to have a "saints' day" (everyone dresses up as his or her patron saint and is prepared to talk about him).

9. Sing the song "The Saints Go Marching in", just for some light treatment of the subject.

10. Ask, "How do you want to be judged when you die? Do you live as you would want to be judged?" Direct students to write down their responses.

## Lesson Plan for a One-day Presentation

1. Pray.

2. Review.

3. Explain about death being the doorway to heaven.

4. Teach about the supremely important duty of loving God and others so as to be ready for death. Use the blackboard (see activites 3 and 7) and tell stories of saints.

5. Describe hell, Purgatory, and heaven. Explain about the Communion of Saints.

6. End the class with pictures or drawings of the lessons.

## Suggested Schedule for a Five-day Presentation

1. Death, doorway to the next life
   *Aim:* to state the real meaning of death and to see the most important goal in life: loving God and others so as to enter heaven.
   *Activities:* see activities 2, 3, and 4.

2. Saints, imitators of Christ and lovers of God
   *Aim:* to show how saints loved God.
   *Activities:* see activities 4 and 8.

3. The Communion of Saints
   *Aim:* to identify and describe heaven, Purgatory, hell, and the Communion of Saints; to be aware of the Last Judgment.
   *Activities:* see activities 5, 7, and 10.

4. Class Mass
   *Aim:* to pray for the holy souls in Purgatory.
   *Activities:* see activity 6.

5. Saints' day
   *Aim:* to become closer to one's patron saint.
   *Activities:* see activity 8.

**Notes:**

# Appendix

## LESSON PLAN OVERVIEW

To plan the year's course, write a title or phrase for the material you are going to cover in a week's time and the pages where the material can be found in the textbook. For example: 1. *Introduction, pp. 9–11.*

1. _____

2. _____

3. _____

4. _____

5. _____

6. _____

7. _____

8. _____

9. _____

10. _____

11. _____

12. _____

13. _____

14. _____

15. _____

16. _____

17. _____

18. _____

19. _____
    _____
20. _____
    _____
21. _____
    _____
22. _____
    _____
23. _____
    _____
24. _____
    _____
25. _____
    _____
26. _____
    _____
27. _____
    _____
28. _____
    _____
29. _____
    _____

30. _____
    _____
31. _____
    _____
32. _____
    _____
33. _____
    _____
34. _____
    _____
35. _____
    _____
36. _____
    _____
37. _____
    _____
38. _____
    _____
39. _____
    _____
40. _____
    _____

# BASIC TRUTHS OF THE CHRISTIAN FAITH

1. *Who created us?*
   God created us.

2. *Who is God?*
   God is the all-perfect Being, Creator and Lord of heaven and earth.

3. *What does "all-perfect" mean?*
   "All-perfect" means that every perfection is found in God, without defect and without limit; in other words it means that he is infinite power, wisdom and goodness.

4. *What does "Creator" mean?*
   "Creator" means that God made all things out of nothing.

5. *What does "Lord" mean?*
   "Lord" means that God is the absolute master of all things.

6. *Does God have a body as we have?*
   No, God does not have a body, for he is a perfectly pure spirit.

7. *Where is God?*
   God is in heaven, on earth, and in every place: he is the unlimited Being.

8. *Has God always existed?*
   Yes, God always has been and always will be: he is the eternal Being.

9. *Does God know all things?*
   Yes, God knows all things, even our thoughts: he is all-knowing.

10. *Can God do all things?*
    God can do all that he wills to do: he is the all-powerful one.

11. *Can God do also something evil?*
    No, God cannot do evil, because he cannot will evil, for he is infinite goodness. But he tolerates evil in order to leave creatures free, and he knows how to bring good even out of evil.

12. *Does God take care of created things?*
    Yes, God takes care of created things and exercises providence over them; he preserves them in existence and directs all of them toward their own proper purposes with infinite wisdom, goodness, and justice.

13. *What purpose did God have in mind when he created us?*
    God created us to know him, to love him and to serve him in this life, and then to enjoy him in the next life, in heaven.

14. *What is heaven?*
    Heaven is the eternal enjoyment of God, who is our happiness, and the enjoyment of all other good things in him, without any evil.

15. *Who merits heaven?*
    Every good person merits heaven—that is, he who loves God, serves him faithfully and dies in his grace.

16. *What do the wicked deserve who do not serve God and who die in mortal sin?*
    The wicked who do not serve God and who die in mortal sin merit hell.

17. *What is hell?*
    Hell is the eternal suffering of the loss of God, who is our happiness. This means a deep and real personal suffering.

18. *Why does God reward the good and punish the wicked?*

God rewards the good and punishes the wicked because he is infinite justice.

19. *Is there only one God?*
There is only one God, but in three equal and distinct Persons, who are the most Holy Trinity.

20. *What are the three Persons of the Holy Trinity called?*
The three Persons of the Holy Trinity are called the Father, the Son, and the Holy Spirit.

21. *Of the three Persons of the Holy Trinity, was one "incarnate", that is, made man?*
Yes, the Second Person, God the Son, became "incarnate", that is, was made man.

22. *What is the Son of God made man called?*
The Son of God made man is called Jesus Christ.

23. *Who is Jesus Christ?*
Jesus Christ is the Second Person of the most Holy Trinity, that is, the Son of God made man.

24. *Is Jesus Christ God and man?*
Yes, Jesus Christ is true God and true man.

25. *Why did the Son of God become man?*
The Son of God became man to save us, that is, to redeem us from sin and to regain heaven for us.

26. *What did Jesus Christ do to save us?*
To save us, Jesus Christ made satisfaction for our sins by suffering and sacrificing himself on the cross, and he taught us how to live according to God's laws.

27. *What must we do to live according to God's laws?*
To live according to God's laws we must believe the truths which he has revealed and observe his commandments, with the help of his grace, which we obtain by means of the sacraments and prayer.

# REVIEW GAMES

Review games are valuable in helping the students to remember the lesson. Students are usually more motivated to memorize things to win a game than to complete a straight memorization assignment. Games can also be used to build confidence (when the teacher gauges the questions to the ability of each student) and cooperation among the students. Often times, the reward of winning is enough for students. However, you might want to give little prizes such as holy cards or medals, etc. The games below will be marked according to the grade level at which they work best: 1° = grades 1–3; 2° = 4–6; and 3° = 7–8.

**Bible Baseball 1°, 2°**

1. Set up bases around the room.

2. Pick teams.

3. Ask a question of a student on one of the teams. If he gets the answer, the student goes to first base and the next student is up for a question. If he misses the answer, he is out. The next teammate must answer the same question. If three students on the same team cannot answer the question or if three questions are missed their team is out and the other team is up.

4. Points are received for "home runs", that is, when a student has gotten to all three bases and reached home base.

**Tic Tac Toe 1°, 2°**

1. Pick sides. "X" goes first.

2. Draw grid on the chalkboard.

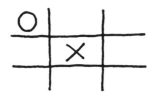

3. Ask a question of a student on the first team. If he answers it correctly, his team chooses where to put the "X". If he answers incorrectly, the other team has a chance to answer the question. If the "O" team answers correctly, they can choose where to put the "O", and then they get their turn. If they answer incorrectly, they merely get their normal turn.

4. The team that gets three "'X's", or three "O's" in a row wins the round. Losers start the next round.

**Peek-a-Boo 2°, 3°**

1. Pick Sides.

2. A student from one team stands at the front of the room with his back to the chalkboard.

3. The teacher writes a word on the board.

4. Teammates can give only one clue to the member at the board. The student at the board chooses which of his teammates will give the clue. A different clue-giver must be chosen for each word.

5. If the student says the word on the board, his team gets a point and the next member of the team gets a chance at the board. If he fails to say the word, the other team gets to play.

## Credo 2°, 3°

*(This game takes a long time.)*

1. Each student plays for himself.

2. Have each student fold a piece of paper in half and cut at the fold.

3. On one half sheet of paper, draw a "CREDO" card (see illustration).

4. Write 25–30 words on the board that relate to the material that you are reviewing; have the students write fill-in-the-blank questions for each word. Assign which word(s) each student will write a question for, so that all the words have a question. Each question should be on a separate piece of paper.

5. Have the students write a word from the board into every box on their "CREDO" cards. No repeats. The middle box is a FREE space.

6. Collect the questions from the students. Mix them up and read a question aloud, twice. If the student has the word on his "CREDO" card, he draws a line through the word, but is careful not to make it unreadable, so that the teacher can

check it if the student wins. Proceed as with a BINGO game.

7. When a student gets a row or black out or four corners he says, "Credo!" If all the words the student crossed out were correct, he must say the words and the questions to the class before he wins.

## Modified "Hangman" 2°, 3°

1. Pick teams (2 or more).

2. Think of a message (or have a list ready beforehand). For example: GOD IS GOOD.

3. Write the spaces for the message on the chalkboard. _____/____/_____.

4. A member from the first team guesses a letter. If he is correct, the team gets a point for every time the letter occurs, for example: if he had guessed a "G" his team would get 2 points (G ____/ ____/G ____) and another member of his team gets to guess the next letter. If he is wrong, write the letter on the board as a letter already used. The turn goes to the next team.

5. If anyone on any team can guess the message before all the letters are in place, he may interrupt and give the answer. His team receives 5 bonus points. If the student guesses incorrectly, his team has 5 points taken away.

6. The team that reaches 100 (or 50, or 25, etc.) first wins. The game can also be played with a time limit instead of a point limit.

**Divine Pursuit 2°, 3°**

Materials: game board (see illustration), a die, tokens (such as figurines of Jesus, Mary, and the saints), plastic or paper chips, cards with catechism questions and answers written on them.

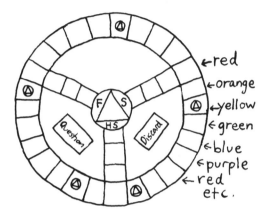

←red
←orange
←yellow
←green
←blue
←purple
←red
etc.

Note: Use six colors for the squares, using each color in succession around the circle and straight paths.

1. Each player (or team) rolls the die. The lowest roll is first. The player to the left is next, etc. Tokens start at the center of the board.

2. To take a turn, roll the die and move the number of spaces indicated on the die. If the person lands on a yellow space, another player draws and asks a question. If the player cannot answer, his turn ends. The correct answer is read aloud and the card put in the discard pile. If the player answers correctly, he receives a red chip and his turn ends. If the player lands on a square of any other color, his turn is over.

3. When a player has obtained three chips, he moves to the center, which must be reached by an exact roll. The player must then answer a question from the pile. If he answers correctly, he has won the game. If not, the player must leave the center on the next turn, and return for another question.

4. When no more questions are left in the question pile, shuffle the discard pile and it will become the question pile again.

# DRAMATIZATION

Dramatization of a scene from Scripture, or the Rosary, etc., helps the students to use all their faculties and senses in learning. For the younger children, you might have to write and produce the play yourself, but older children (grades 3–8) can make and produce the play themselves. Thus, the students use their imagination and creativity as well as their senses. Below are three ways you can dramatize a scene.

## Popsicle Stick Puppets and Shoe Box Theater

The puppets are easily made from popsicle sticks and either felt, construction paper, or cut out pictures. For example:

For the theater, take a large shoe box and cut two slots, one toward the top of the box on one of the long sides, and the other toward the bottom of the box on the opposite long side (the slot toward the top will be where you insert the puppets; the slot toward the bottom will be for inserting the backdrop, or scenery).

## Masks

To identify the different characters in a play without having to make elaborate costumes, it is quite easy to make masks. For example, if you wanted to dramatize the temptation and fall of man, you could make the following masks out of paper and have the students color them, or make them out of construction paper.

EVE    ADAM    GOD    SERPENT    ANGEL

## Costumes and Props

Costumes do not have to be elaborate to be effective. An old sheet, bathrobe, or remnants of material are usually all you need. If you need a crown and a miter these can be made out of construction paper and sized to fit the head of the actor. For example:

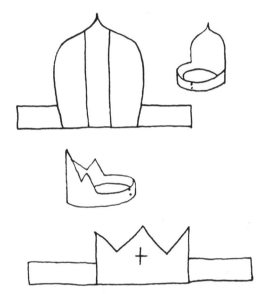

To show the change from perfect happiness to the fallen state of Adam and Eve, or the original delight of Satan at man's fall, then disappointment at God's promise, make the masks reversible. The masks may be hand-held and then flipped at the proper time during the play. For example:

Adam before the Fall.

Adam after the Fall

Beards too are easily made of paper, then hooked around the ears:

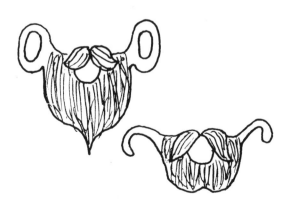

Swords can be cut out from cardboard and covered with aluminum foil, and chains can be made by linking paper strips together.

(Chains and swords might be used for a play on Joan of Arc or on Joseph being sold into slavery, etc.)

# Commandment mobile

Materials needed:
cardboard or poster paper
crayons
string
wire hangers

Use crossed hangers

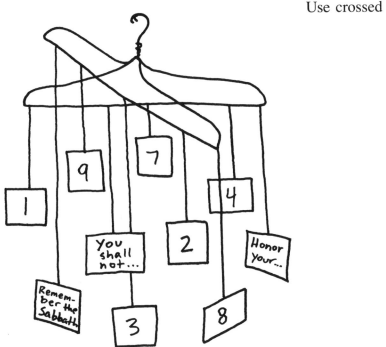

Have the students write each of the Commandments on a card
and put the number of the Commandment on the other side. This
may be decorated or illustrated. Then they should punch a hole in
each card and suspend it from the hangers with string.

# Grade 3 Activity Book Answer Key

*N.B.*: Many of the questions require the student to give an answer in his own words. Where specific doctrinal or historical points that the student is expected to learn in this course of studies are looked for, suggested answers (or outlines) are provided to the teacher. In other places, the student is expected to write a response for which no specific answer is needed. A note is provided to indicate that answers will vary.

Students should answer in complete sentences.

## Chapter 1

1. eternal, beginning, end; 2. precious; 3. image; 4. soul; 5. love; 6. God; 7. Our Father, Lord's Prayer.

## Chapter 3

1. Jesus; 2. Bible; 3. Tradition; 4. Word of God; 5. Scriptures.

## Chapter 4

1. pure spirits who are smarter and more powerful than we are; 2. to serve God; 3. they had a choice; 4. promised to send a Savior; 5. Holy Baptism.

## Chapter 5

"**Jacob** of *God* the and, **Isaac** of *God* the, **Abraham** of *God* the *I am*"
Answer: "**I am the God of Abraham, the God of Isaac, the God of Jacob.**"

## Chapter 6

1. Covenant; 2. Moses; 3. Passover; 4. Egyptians; 5. Canaan;   6. Abraham;   7. Commandments; 8. true.

## Chapter 7

*In order, going downward*:
shepherd, Lord, pastures, restful, soul
my, right, His, dark, You
I, me, anoint, oil, cup
want, goodness, life, dwell, house.

## Chapter 8

1. the Ten Commandments; 2. on our hearts; 3. worship and respect God; 4. be kind and fair to each other; 5. the joys of Heaven that last for ever;

## Chapter 9

I.

*Circled:* loving God above all else; learning about God; serving God; believing in God; listening to God; adoring Our Lord; saying the Apostles' Creed.

*X through:* being superstitious; doubting God; thinking only about money.

II.

*Circled:* speaking about God lovingly; thanking and praising God; keeping a promise; asking God's help; reverently making the Sign of the Cross; praying; honoring Mary and all the saints.

*X through:* making irreverent fun of God or anyone; deliberately causing disturbance at Mass or in Church; using God's name in anger.

## Chapter 11

*Going downward*:
III, V, V, III, IV, V, IV, III, V, IV, III, IV.

## Chapter 12

1. holy, baptism; 2. respect; 3. modest; 4. faithful; 5. property; 6. steal; 7. honest; 8. witness, truth; 9. integrity; heaven; 11. fool

## Chapter 13

1. God . . . is the only One who essentially forgives our sins.
2. Peter . . . denied Jesus three times on the night He was betrayed. He wept with sorrow.
3. The lost sheep . . . was known by name and was precious to the shepherd in the same way we are loved by God.
4. No sin on earth . . . is greater than God's love and mercy.

5. Jesus gave the apostles . . . the power to forgive sins in His name.

6. Sins . . . are not all equal. Some are more serious than others.

7. Mary Magdalen . . . poured precious oil on Jesus' feet and wept for forgiveness.

8. The sacrament of Penance . . . frees us from our sins.

9. Mortal sin and venial sin . . . are two kinds of actual sin.

10. Our priests today . . . carry the same power as the apostles to forgive sins.

## Chapter 14

1. sorry; 2. Penance; 3. Contrition; 4. sorrow; 5. sin; 6. accept; 7. Spirit; 8. love; 9. forgiving; 10. absolution; 11. priest; 12. intention; 13. Reconciliation; 14. Amen.

## Chapter 16

*Across*:
1. hidden
3. Jesus
6. Jewish
7. lives
9. Nazareth
10. God
11. baptized
12. other

*Down*:
2. dove
3. John
4. Spirit
5. mission
6. Joseph
8. carpenter
10. God

## Chapter 17

*Going downward*:
f, g, e, b, d, h, j, i, a, c.

## Chapter 18

"This is the body of me . . . this is the blood of me. . . ."

"touto estin to soma mou . . . touto estin to haima mou. . . ."

## Chapter 19

Answers will vary.

## Chapter 20

1. completely; 2. shed; 3. priests; 4. Temple; 5. gave; 6. Mass; 7. offered; 8. New; 9. altar.

## Chapter 21

*Going downward*:
3, 9, 7, 5, 1, 8, 6, 2, 4, 10.

## Chapter 22

*Going downward*:
4, 9, 6, 5, 3, 7, 2, 8, 1.

## Chapter 23

Answers will vary.

## Chapter 24

1. love; 2. hungers; 3. receive; 4. thanksgiving; 5. attention; 6. grace; 7. time; 8. souls; 9. invite.

## Chapter 25

*Across*:
1. forty
3. sits
4. at
6. garden
7. away
8. empty
9. ghost
11. alive
12. afraid
15. Jesus
16. Resurrection
18. hand
21. cross
22. dead
23. hope

*Down*:
2. third
3. stone
4. always
5. Mary
8. Easter
10. heaven
11. apostles
13. locked
14. ascended
15. joy
17. rejoice
19. God

## Chapter 27

1. Church; 2. apostles; 3. Peter; 4. Christ; 5. bishops; 6. lives; 7. priests; 8. sacrifices; 9. called; 10. other; 11. build; 12. martyrs; 13. actions; 14. Catholic

## Chapter 29

Hail Mary, full of grace!
The Lord is with thee.
Blessed art thou among women,
and blessed is the fruit of thy womb, Jesus.
Holy Mary, Mother of God,
pray for us sinners,
now and at the hour of our death.
Amen.